PETER H. JOHNSTON

THE UNIVERSITY AT ALBANY—STATE UNIVERSITY OF NEW YORK

Opening Minds

Using Language to Change Lives

STENHOUSE PUBLISHERS • PORTLAND, MAINE

Stenhouse Publishers
www.stenhouse.com

Credits

The author draws extensively from, and gratefully acknowledges, Maria Nichols's *Comprehension Through Conversation: The Power of Purposeful Talk in the Reading Workshop* (Heinemann, 2006) and Mary Cowhey's *Black Ants and Buddhists: Thinking Critically and Teaching Differently in the Primary Grades* (Stenhouse, 2006).

Pages 7 and 80: Cartoons by Betsy Streeter. Used with permission. www.betsystreeter.com.

Page 41: Figure 4.1 © Alex Gregory/The New Yorker Collection/ www.cartoonbank.com.

Library of Congress Cataloging-in-Publication Data
Johnston, Peter H.
    Opening minds : using language to change lives / Peter H. Johnston.
    p. cm.
    Includes bibliographical references and index.
    ISBN 978-1-57110-816-6 (pbk. : alk. paper)
    ISBN 978-1-57110-953-8 (ebook)
    1. Children—Language. 2. Oral communication. 3. Interaction analysis in education. 4. Verbal behavior. 5. Sociolinguistics. I. Title.
    LB1139.L3.J636 2012
    372.6—dc23
                                                                    2011037288

Cover design, interior design, and typesetting by Martha Drury
Manufactured in the United States of America

PRINTED ON 30% PCW
RECYCLED PAPER

20 19   9 8

This book is dedicated to all the remarkable teachers I have had the privilege of learning from. Most recently:

Susie Althof
Kathy Champeau
Mary Cowhey
Cheryl Dozier
Amy Faulkner
Liz Hill
Gay Ivey
Pegeen Jensen
Jeralyn Johnson
Tina Johnston
Brian Lundstrom
Maria Nichols
Beth Teachey
Trudy Warner

It is also dedicated to the memory of John G. Nicholls.

Contents

Acknowledgments

I set out to write a book that expanded the themes introduced in *Choice Words*—the idea that the language we use in teaching can have profound effects on children's development. When I was halfway through writing the book I encountered several things at once. I spent time learning from Pegeen Jensen in her first-grade classroom and talking with Liz Yanoff, at the time a doctoral student, who was doing research for her dissertation in Pegeen's classroom. I also read Maria Nichols's book *Comprehension Through Conversation*. I found the conversations in it to be exciting and about much more than comprehension. So I contacted Maria, and she took me to Webster Elementary School in San Diego, where I was privileged to meet and spend time in the classrooms of Susie Althof and Jeralyn Johnson. This led, the following spring, to working with Maria to videotape Susie's and Jeralyn's teaching with the intention of producing a videobook (which, regrettably, this book has delayed). I learned more than I can say from these teachers and Maria. Maria has since written two more excellent books from which I have also learned: *Talking About Text* and *Expanding Comprehension with Multigenre Text Sets*. I have drawn on each of these in the present book.

These books essentially offer records of what really capable teachers do and say. I find that they fit very well with other research, and where they don't, it's because the other researchers haven't caught up. Martha Horn and Mary Ellen Giacobbe's book *Talking, Drawing, Writing* shows in exquisite detail how to talk with very young writers. Similarly, Katie Wood Ray's *About the Authors* with Lisa Cleaveland and *Already Ready* with Matt Glover offer particularly good examples of teacher talk. Another influential book has been Mary Cowhey's *Black Ants and Buddhists*—an inspiring account of her teaching critical literacy in a first/second-grade classroom. Mary allowed me to visit her classroom, and both the book and the visit strongly affected my thinking, as you will see. Earlier than this, my thinking on critical literacy was influenced by Kathy and Randy Bomer's book *For a Better World*. When it comes to books directly about the language we use with children, Ruth Charney's book *Teaching Children to Care* was similarly influential. It is a handbook no teacher should be without.

Two other researchers have been particularly influential in my thinking. You will see the pervasive and long-term influence of Carol Dweck's work, which I have admired since I was a graduate student and she was an assistant professor at the University of Illinois. I thoroughly recommend reading her books *Mindset* and *Self-Theories*. In recent years, I have also closely followed the work of Neil Mercer—try his books *Words and Minds* and *Exploring Talk in School*.

Many conversations with teacher Kathy Champeau in recent years have stimulated—and knocked the edges off—my thinking. More recently I began working with Gay Ivey. Gay's work with middle school students showed me the power of engagement and increased my commitment to broader views of literacy, education, and children's development. She has helped me see just how right John Dewey was.

If I have anything useful to say about teaching and learning it is because of what I have learned from all of these people. To each of you, I hope you understand that I can't thank you enough.

My colleagues at the University at Albany have also played their part. While it was regrettably necessary for me to become department chair, they have made it easier for me to fulfill my responsibilities in that role (to the extent that I have). Our department secretary, Linda Papa, has saved my bacon on many occasions. Conversations about research and teaching in the department have certainly played a role in my thinking. For all this, I owe thanks to Stephanie Affinito, Cheryl Dozier, Ginny Goatley, Jolene Malavasic, Linda Papa, Donna Scanlon, Sean Walmsley, Margi Sheehy, Kelly Wissman, and Rose Marie Weber.

I want to thank Philippa Stratton, editor and outstanding educator, for her patience with my work and for her remarkable impact on the field. Philippa is the unsung heroine of professional reading for teachers.

Finally, I want to thank Tina, my dear wife of thirty-three joyful years, without whom life would be pale. "On with the dance!"

CHAPTER 1

Choosing Words, Choosing Worlds

Children seldom misquote you. They usually repeat word for word what you shouldn't have said.

—Unknown

One summer at a family reunion, I went to chat with two of my nieces, ages three and five, who were playing in the sandbox. As I sat down, they greeted me as follows:

> **Amelia:** Here's Uncle Peter. Let's play. I'll be the mother.
> **Marie:** Yeah, I'll be the little daughter. Uncle Peter can be your husband.
> **Amelia:** No. We're not married yet.

This brief interaction captures for me something familiar about language and schooling. In seconds, with a handful of words, and with my relatively passive consent, the girls constructed a world in which we might live for a time—they decided who we would and would not be and what we would be doing. Classrooms are just like this. As teachers, we choose our words and, in the process, construct the classroom worlds for our students and ourselves. The worlds we construct offer opportunities and constraints. Indeed, a few minutes later in the sandbox, driving a steel truck along an imaginary road, Marie lamented, "I need a bigger road." Looking up she saw the edge of the sandbox and said, with some frustration, "I need a bigger world."

Recognizing the limitations of the world we have constructed is important, but not always easy. Marie had the advantage of seeing the world she had constructed in the context of the larger world beyond. In this book, I show you some different worlds that we construct in the classroom, what is possible and not possible in those worlds, and how we construct them using the tools of our language.

Sometimes a single word changes everything. Robin, a local teacher, asked her colleagues if they had advice on how to cook a wild turkey. Her husband had hit the bird with his truck and he had brought it home for his wife to prepare. Several colleagues offered advice and recipes, but one bystander pointed out that the bird was in fact "road kill." Robin prepared the turkey according to the recipes, but she couldn't eat it. Once it had been named as road kill, everything changed. In classrooms, events happen, but their meaning only becomes apparent through the filter of the language in which we immerse them. Children don't know whether something is a gourmet feast or road kill until their attention is drawn to markers that tell them which world they are in. Introducing a spelling test to a student by saying, "Let's see how many words you know," is different from saying, "Let's see how many words you know already." It is only one word, but the *already* suggests that any words the child knows are ahead of expectation and, most important, that there is nothing permanent about what is known and not known.

A Moment of Teaching

One morning I was in a friend's first-grade classroom. Pegeen (rhymes with Colleen; red hair, Irish) was reading *Snowflake Bentley* by Jacqueline Briggs Martin with the children, an appropriate book under the circumstances. It was February, and what would become eight inches of snow was falling, complicating the morning commute. Everything was late. As Pegeen was reading, a teacher aide assigned to one of the children arrived, late. Pegeen looked up and greeted her, returned to the children and said, "I just made a big mistake as a reader. I got distracted when someone came into the room. So I'm going to reread this section here."

One of her students, Michael, said, "That happens to me too."

"Say more about that," Pegeen responded.

"Well, I go back and read a bit . . ." and he added a little detail.

Fifteen minutes later there was a brief disruption to the class, and Pegeen reminded them, "What did Michael say? Remember? Go back to the spot and start over."

Two days later, in the middle of independent reading, one of the children observed, "I need to reread 'cause I just got distracted."

There is something very ordinary about this set of interactions. Yet, it captures at once the simplicity and the complexity of the language we use with children. None of Pegeen's comments was strictly necessary. And yet, when she said, "I just made a big mistake as a reader. I got distracted when someone came into the room. So I'm going to reread this section here," she did two really important things. First, she leveled the power difference between teacher and students. She said, "I make mistakes just like you." Second, her comment began to explain the meaning of errors. When you make a mistake, it means nothing more than that. Fix it. Learn from it. It does not mean you are incompetent, stupid, or not a good person.

Not all first graders—or adults—know this. However, if Pegeen's first graders don't learn this lesson, they will not be able to risk taking on learning challenges for fear of making mistakes. And, if they do make a mistake, they won't be able to talk about it. This would not only deprive the teacher of her most useful assessment information, but it would deprive the class of the opportunity to rehearse agentive narratives— narratives that position them as people who can act and have an impact: "(When I make the mistake of getting distracted) I go back and read a bit (and that fixes it)." Errors usually happen at the edge of what we can do, when we are stretching into new territory—when we are learning.

Pegeen's "Say more about that" is also less ordinary than it seems. First, it is her best assessment tool. It often lets her know what the children are thinking. At the same time, it gave Michael the sense that he had something to say and, since Pegeen and the other students listened to him, he got the sense that he was respected. This sense was reinforced when Pegeen reminded the children later, "What did Michael say? . . ." She didn't need to say this. She could have just reminded them of the strategy without attributing it to Michael. If giving an accurate account was the point, it was Pegeen, not Michael, who mentioned the strategy. But it was an opportunity for her to position Michael—that is, to create a story line in which Michael was a particular kind of person. Michael was not one of the most capable readers in the class, but her comment deputized him as the sort of guy who knew something about strategy use and as someone who was worth listening to. He was definitely a guy who contributed to the conversation. Legitimizing student comments like this, not judging them, encourages students to make more contributions to classroom thinking, which in turn offers more opportunities to position students in productive narratives.

This set of interactions might not mean much by itself, but the threads it contains, repeated over and over in different forms, moment to moment, day to day, week to week, month to month, start to amount to something. Their power is strengthened as they echo and reverberate in the children's talk, as we saw two days later when one of the girls noticed she was distracted and needed to fix the problem by rereading. She thought this to herself, forgetting that her mouth was still engaged, thus announcing it to the world. Her announcement rehearsed the strategy, offered another opportunity for peers to learn it, and reinforced Pegeen's assertion that mistakes are nothing to be ashamed of. The students thus took over the narrative, and Pegeen's words resonated through the children's learning lives. The goals the children choose, what they value, the feelings they experience, the identities and relationships they take up, the theories they hold about learning, ideas, and people, are all touched by Pegeen's choice of words. Her words change the life of the classroom. They change the worlds the children inhabit, and consequently who they can be, what they will feel, what they can know, and what will be normal behavior.

Teaching is planned opportunism. We have an idea of what we want to teach children, and we plan ways to make that learning possible. When we put our plans into action, children offer us opportunities to say something, or not, and the choices we make affect what happens next. Teaching requires constant improvisation. It is jazz. A child asks a question. Do we answer it? If so, how? How long do we wait before we answer it? If not, what do we say? A child successfully accomplishes something—or fails to. We have another opportunity to say something, but what? My intention with this book is to offer a basis for choosing more productive talk—how to make the most of those opportunities children offer us. More important, I hope to show you that, given that we are playing conversational jazz, it is important that we choose a productive key in which to improvise.

Teaching for Now and for the Future

Third graders Manny and Sergio are sitting discussing a book together.[1] The book is *A Picnic in October* by Eve Bunting. The story is written from the perspective of a young boy who is dragged along with his family each October to the Statue of Liberty for a picnic to celebrate his grandmother's passage into the country. The boy misbehaves, but at the end of the book, he sees the way another couple looks at the statue and he changes his perspective.

> **Manny:** No, no, you see, he was rude, but he changed.
>
> **Sergio:** Rude people don't change. He was making fun of everyone; he pretended to throw up . . .
>
> **Manny:** That's sick!
>
> **Sergio:** Yeah, but it was because he didn't want to go, he was like mad that they made him . . . and embarrassed too, like me when my mom makes me go . . .
>
> **Manny:** Yeah, at first, but look here at the end, see (*flips the pages*)—they're leaving, . . . here it is . . . see, he looks, he looks at the other family—it's like he gets it!
>
> **Sergio:** Let me see again (*grabs book, studies the pictures on the pages Manny showed him, and whisper-reads the words on the pages*). Oh—you mean like now he gets why the Grandma thinks the statue is a big deal?
>
> **Manny:** Yeah, now he gets it.
>
> **Sergio:** So now it's in his heart, too?
>
> **Manny:** No—well OK, yeah, I guess it could be in his heart, but now he really gets that it's in his grandma's heart.

Several features of this conversation strike me as significant. These children are fully engaged in discussing a book—without a teacher. They are choosing to discuss it and make connections to their own lives. They each have an interpretation of the text, but they are not wedded to that particular interpretation. They disagree with each other and take each other's position very seriously, feeling the need to justify their own position using evidence from the text. Each uses the difference in perspective to expand his own understanding. These children are actually in control of their own development. They don't need the teacher for this (now)—but they need each other. They are in control of their own development because they know how to engage each other (and a book) in such a way that it expands their minds. They understand the value of difference.

These reasons alone would be enough to justify the dialogic teaching that makes these interactions possible, so we will look carefully at dialogic teaching in this book. But in the course of conversations like

Manny and Sergio's, these children and their peers are learning how to participate in a strong democracy. They expect to engage, to disagree, and to grow from that disagreement. At some point, they will vote, but that will be after they have understood their own and each other's views and expanded their collective mind in the process. Even if they vote self-interest, it will be enlightened self-interest. They will have a sense of how their self-interest is tied to the interests of the larger community.

There is evidence that interactions like those between Manny and Sergio, and the teaching that leads to them, develop the children's social imagination—their ability to empathize, and to imagine others' thinking. This ability, in turn, increases the probability of healthy moral development; it reduces the likelihood that they will stereotype, it expands their social networks, and it enhances the way they view each other. It also makes them less likely to misbehave at home or at school. Of course, if you are only interested in bluntly academic learning, rest assured that Manny and Sergio are also developing their reading comprehension ability. Also rest assured that the teacher, who can count on Manny and Sergio learning independently together, is freed to work more closely with students who need some focused attention.

Children in classrooms like Manny and Sergio's take these ways of thinking about what they are doing, the relationships and ways of responding to difference, as normal and view themselves and each other through them. They slowly come to embody the interactions—like a dancer's muscles come to own and remember dances. This embodiment is less visible than the smile (or frown) lines with which we shape our faces, but more deeply embedded. A college graduate who had been in such a classroom in elementary school had this to say on reflection:

> There was a time in high school where I hit a slump and I had a moment of self-evaluation as to why I felt that way. I realized learning wasn't fun anymore for me; I had to sit down and remember when it was. The [dialogic classroom] period was that for me. That experience gave me something to look back on to remember and hold on to. I told my mother that [dialogic classroom] introduced me to that state of mind that loved to learn. That passion and thirst for learning was one of the many things that is still with me today . . . my whole thought process was shaped from that one significant period in my life.[2]

Because of our embodied histories, much of the time our own responses to children are automatic. We open our mouths and our parents or our previous teachers come out. Changing our talk requires gaining a sense of what we are doing, our options, their consequences, and why we make the choices we make. In this book, I show you how our values, our beliefs, and our histories, and the context in which we work, have an impact on the language we choose. I also show you that our language choices have serious consequences for children's learning and for who they become as individuals and as a community. I help you make productive choices, because the language we choose in our teaching changes the worlds children inhabit now and those they will build in the future. Make no mistake, when we are teaching for today, we are teaching into tomorrow.

CHAPTER 2

Learning Worlds: People, Performing, and Learning

Language has the power to shape our consciousness; and it does so
for each human child, by providing the theory that he or she uses to
interpret and manipulate their environment.

—MICHAEL HALLIDAY[1]

A first grader in writing workshop observed, "I'm not very good at this poetry stuff. I think I'm gonna stick with nonfiction." His teacher asked how he could possibly know that. He replied, "I don't know. I'm just not good at it." The finality of his assertion is disturbing. He is not saying, "I'm not good at it *yet*." He expects not to be good at it now and forever. At six, he concludes that further attempts at poetry will be futile. He's just not a poetry kind of guy. In what world is it possible for a six-year-old to know this with such certainty?[2] A middle school student observed, "Some kids are born good readers and some kids aren't. I've always been a bad reader and I always will be. It's too late for me,"[3] a conclusion that is equally final but more generally debilitating than the first grader's.

Most of us have encountered students making comments like these and we do our best to change their minds. Adela Laczynski,[4] reflecting on early teaching experiences, heard one of her students say "I'm dumb, I'm dumb, I'm dumb, I'm dumb, I'm dumb." Appalled, she immediately tried to persuade him otherwise, telling him he was smart and asking

9

him to say so too, but he wouldn't. The next day she took a more aggressive approach to changing this self-talk. She instructed his group to say "I am smart and I can read" ten times, for which they would get a reward. They obliged her, but she felt conflicted. She said it felt like saying "Here's $5, kid, go buy yourself some self-esteem." "But," she asks, "What else can I do?"

Answering this question requires understanding that the problem is not centrally about self-esteem. The problem is that these students live in a world of permanent traits and (in)abilities. They believe that people have fixed, unchanging characteristics. They think some people are good at poetry (or math, or reading) and some are not. Some are smart, some are not, and there really isn't much they can do about it. In this world, simple events, like mistakes or unsuccessful attempts, are indicators of those fixed characteristics.

Like Adela, often we try to boost these children's self-esteem by convincing them that they really are smart (or good readers, or good at poetry). Unfortunately, by continuing the smart-dumb conversation, we actually confirm the children's belief in fixed characteristics. Smart is just the other end of the dumb conversation, and by affirming that someone is smart, we agree that smart-dumb is the way to think about people. We might even point to the child's successes as evidence that he is smart. But if successes can be indicators of smartness, then failures, errors, or struggles can be evidence of stupidness. Heaping such praise upon these students to build their self-esteem won't solve the problem, it will only deepen it.

Let's take the "I'm-not-good-at-poetry" student. I'm certain his teacher never said to him or anyone else, "You're not good at this." However, there's a good chance that when he successfully finished his nonfiction writing, someone said to him, "You're really good at this." Knowing that writers are either good or not good, when his first attempt at poetry was not as successful as his nonfiction experience, he might reasonably conclude that he's just not good at poetry. Nobody had to tell him that. They just had to make it clear that writers come in two kinds—good at it and not.

The consequences of viewing people as having fixed attributes, such as being smart or not, are well researched. Referring to these studies, I want to show you how simple comments like "You're good at this" or "You must be smart" help create a world that we might not want to live in because of its academic, emotional, relational, and moral landscape. It is, in fact, the "dark side." We have quite detailed maps of this world and we know the language that opens the portal to it.

Fortunately, research also shows us how to construct a much more productive world. I will introduce you to both, and show you why particular words can open or close the doors to each.

Children's Theories About Being Smart or Becoming Smart

Carol Dweck and her colleagues have studied children's theories of intelligence—what children think it means to be smart. Some children view ability, or intelligence, as if it were a general character trait, something people have more or less of, usually from birth.[5] We'll call this theorizing fixed theorizing because it represents characteristics as permanent—some people are just not as smart as others and there's not much they can do about it. When people view life through a dynamic theory, on the other hand, they think of ability, or intelligence, as something that grows with learning and depends on the situation.[6] A dynamic theorist thinks that the more you learn, the smarter you get. A fixed theorist thinks, "I'm not a good writer." A dynamic theorist thinks, "I'm not very good at writing poetry *yet*," or, "I'm not very good at writing in very noisy situations *yet*."

Holding a fixed theory or a dynamic theory may seem like no big deal. In fact, when children are being successful, you can't easily tell the difference between those holding one or the other theory. When people run into difficulties, though, their theories matter, big time. When children holding fixed theories encounter difficulties, mistakes become crippling. Worse, if they think that a task might be difficult, they choose not to even try so that they won't fail and maybe look stupid. They choose not to try even if it means losing an opportunity to learn something important. They choose, instead, to look good, or at least not look bad, at whatever it is they are doing. They choose performance goals. If you ask them "When do you feel smart?" they say something like "When I do better than the others" or "When I finish first" or "When I don't make any mistakes" or "When the others are struggling but it's easy for me."[7]

This belief in fixed personal characteristics and choice of performance goals is very well researched and very persistent.[8] Since I will be referring to it a great deal, I will simply call it the *fixed-performance frame*, for fixed theory and performance goals.

The world of dynamic theorizing is very different. At the beginning of the year in Jean Cardanay's second-grade class, the students were heading off to lunch. As James walked past me, he confessed, "This is really hard. It's much harder than first grade." I noticed that he didn't look unhappy about it though. In fact, there was a hint of excitement and satisfaction on his face. So I responded, "But fun though?" He nodded vigorously. We expect this response from someone with a dynamic theory. In the dynamic world, the more you learn, the smarter you get, and though it can involve hard work, learning is the goal. Looking good or bad is not especially relevant. So when you ask dynamic theorists "When do you feel smart?" they say something like "When I'm doing some hard math problems" or "When I figure it out by myself" or "When I'm teaching someone else."[9]

Dynamic theorists can afford to take on challenge because in their world, mistakes don't point to fixed and shameful inadequacies. In a dynamic world, when you run into difficulty it just means things are becoming more interesting. Challenging activities present no threat, only the promise of learning something new. The dynamic theory world is more interesting and less anxiety producing than the one constructed from fixed theories. Because people holding a dynamic view of human behavior generally choose learning goals, my shorthand for this pattern will be the *dynamic-learning frame*.

Theories and Consequences

To make the difference between fixed-performance and dynamic-learning frames concrete, let me describe a series of experimental studies designed to explore these worlds. Claudia Meuller and Carol Dweck took fifth graders out of their classroom, one at a time, and had them do an easy nonverbal reasoning test. When some of the students finished the test they were told, "This is your score. It's a very good score. You must have worked hard." Researchers told the other students, "This is your score. It's a very good score. You must be smart." They were then told they were going to do more of the tests during the day but that they could choose the next one. They could choose an easy one like the first one or "one that's hard but you might learn something from it." The researchers wanted to know which students would choose to take on challenge in the interest of learning, and which would choose safety even at the cost of not learning. Would telling children they were smart boost their self-esteem and enable them to take on the challenge? Not at all. Only about a third of the you-must-be-smart group chose to struggle and learn, whereas better than 90 percent of the you-must-have-worked-hard students chose to take up the challenge and learn. The single piece of feedback created for some students a world in which working hard gets results, and in which errors and successes say nothing about them personally, except that, in this situation, they worked hard and it paid off. Only 35 percent of the you-must-be-smart students chose to take up the challenge. They had been led into a world in which people are smart or not smart, period, in which doing the puzzles is about deciding who is and is not smart, and in which people can determine this from a single test score.

Ninety percent versus 35 percent willing to take up challenge in order to learn is a big difference. By itself, that might be enough to persuade me not to give feedback that opens the door to the fixed-performance world. But there's more.

The students next did a hard test on which they all struggled. Then they were asked how much they liked working on the problems, how much they would like to take some problems home to work on, and why they thought they did badly. The students who got the "smart" feedback enjoyed the problems less and were less interested in taking any home. They were also more likely to explain their performance in terms of fixed ability rather than in terms of effort, over which they have some control.

And there's even more to the study. The students next did an easy test like the first one. On this test, the "worked-hard" students actually did better than they did on the first test, whereas the "smart" students did worse. Finally, the researchers told the children that students in other schools would be doing these puzzles too, and invited them to write a letter to tell those other students what it's like to do the puzzles. On the form they used to write the letter, there was a little space for the students to enter their test score. And here's the kicker. Forty percent of the "smart" students—those in the fixed-performance world—lied about their score. Because in that world their score reflected a deep and permanent trait, they inflated their score to impress people—people whom they would never even meet. Only one of the "worked-hard" students did this. In other words, a single comment can profoundly change the academic and moral choices children make. It literally changes the world they live in.

In another study, researchers induced children to take up fixed or dynamic theories and then arranged for them to do badly on a test.[10] The children were then offered the opportunity to look at another student's test paper. They could choose a student who did worse than them on the test or a student who did better than them. Those with a dynamic-learning view chose to look at the work of students who had done better, so they too could learn how to do the problems better. Students with fixed-performance theories, however, chose to view the work of students who did worse so they could feel better about their own performance. They chose to look better to themselves at the cost of learning nothing.

In a fixed-performance world, there is nothing to be done about one's learning. When Erin McCloskey challenged a high school special education student to work with her on a poem, he said, "Why does it matter? Nothing helps me anyway. People are good at some things and bad at others."[11] In his view, tutoring simply offered him more opportunities to show how bad he was at reading and writing, which he couldn't change. Special education is particularly good at opening the door to the fixed-performance world. It is a world of presumed permanent disabling traits. Special education students are not only placed within a fixed-performance frame but also are given frequent evidence that they are not being successful, a combination that is particularly problematic.

In other words, the problem is self-perpetuating. Students in a fixed-performance frame who believe they are unsuccessful make decisions that diminish their likelihood of succeeding in the future. Consider a study by Ying-Yi Hong and her colleagues in which they persuaded some students to adopt a fixed-performance frame and others to adopt a dynamic-learning frame before taking a nonverbal reasoning test.[12] After the test, regardless of their score, half were told they did well and half that they did badly. The students were then offered a tutorial class that would help them to do better on the next tests. Three quarters of the students in the dynamic-learning frame opted to take the tutorial. Whether or not they thought they were successful made no difference; the tutorial was an opportunity to learn.

Many fewer students in the fixed-performance frame chose to take the tutorial. Sixty percent of those led to believe they did well chose to take the tutorial. Of those who thought they did badly, only 13 percent chose to take it.[13] In a fixed-performance frame, those who most needed the tutorial chose not to take it, because doing so might have revealed to others their (fixed) incompetence. Besides, if you're permanently not good at something and you don't enjoy it, where's the benefit?

Agency and Helplessness

Children who adopt a fixed-performance frame tend to become help-less when they run into trouble. They cease being strategic—except when it comes to ego-defense.

Taking up the fixed-performance narrative affects the way we expe-rience the world and ourselves. When we encounter difficulty, we attribute it to our permanent characteristics. We say things like "I've never been good at this sort of thing" or "I have a terrible memory" or (perhaps only in our heads) "I guess I'm not very smart." When we find ourselves publicly facing difficulty, we sometimes place blame for our difficulties on someone or something else: "You shouldn't have put the problems so close together" or "You interrupted my thinking." Where possible, we try to avoid challenging tasks in which we might struggle and make mistakes, and thus provide evidence of our incompetence. We choose tasks that are easy enough that we're guaranteed success but just hard enough for us to look good.

Having taken up the fixed-performance narrative, we tend to live into it, becoming the character with the fatal flaw. Not only do children who adopt a fixed-performance frame become helpless when they encounter failure, but when they subsequently face problems that they had previously solved, they believe they might not be able to solve them a second time and, indeed, they don't do as well as they did previously.[14] In fact, they essentially abandon being productively strategic and shift any strategic efforts to ego-defensive behaviors, such as placing blame or trying to distract attention with tales of their successes in other areas. Encountering failure affects how they feel about themselves, about their experience, and about their future. It even affects their memory. They recall not being as successful as they in fact had been. For example, in one study, even though students had been successful on eight different problems and unsuccessful on only two, those adopting a fixed-performance frame recalled being successful on five and unsuc-cessful on six.[15]

Children who adopted a dynamic theory behaved the opposite way. They were confident that they could solve the problems again and they recalled their degree of success accurately. They didn't blame their intellect or anyone else for any lack of success—or even consider them-selves to be failing. Instead, when they ran into trouble they gave them-selves instructions and reviewed what they knew that might help them. In short, they acted strategically. Children in a dynamic-learning frame actually use deeper processing when reading difficult material and they become more rather than less strategic when they encounter difficulty.

Figure 2.1 summarizes the beliefs linked to the dynamic-learning and fixed-performance frameworks. There are essentially three different aspects. One is the belief in a fixed versus dynamic view of ability or intelligence. The second is the choice of performance versus learning goals. The third is the meaning children make of different events when they view them through one or the other belief system, and the consequent focus of their attention. In a dynamic view, the process—*how* they did things—is most important. From a fixed view, the process is of little consequence; it is the outcome, the performance, the speed, and the number of errors that draw most attention, because they represent the otherwise hidden amount of ability.

Given this information, I'm sure it will come as no surprise that students classified as having learning disabilities are more likely to adopt a fixed frame with respect to ability than are students classified as not having disabilities. The disabled students (this belief system truly is disabling) view increased effort as simply providing evidence of their lack of ability. They are also more inclined to adopt performance goals. It is their adoption of the fixed frame and their diminished sense of agency that lie at the heart of the problem.[16]

I want to emphasize that these different frames are found not only in school. They are in the culture at large—that's why they're in our heads. In a recent survey, Kathy Champeau and I asked parents whether high-stakes testing had impacted their children or their home life and if so, how.[17] We were struck by the extent to which the stories they offered showed the effects of fixed-performance theorizing:

> *My second grader was emotionally distraught crying and traumatized over having to take the test, "Mom, I just want to be stupid and not take the test." My 5th grader has no self-esteem, deems herself as stupid and has been led to believe she's never going to graduate from school or be anything in life because she's not smart. She totally shut down emotionally and educationally. Yet both kids bring home A's and B's.*

And:

> *My child becomes argumentative, moody and generally upset when standardized testing times roll around. [She] thinks she's stupid because she didn't pass the tests for math and reading, yet her teachers*

Figure 2.1 Dynamic-Learning Beliefs and Fixed-Performance Beliefs

Belief System Frames

Dynamic-Learning Frame	Fixed-Performance Frame
The more you learn, the smarter you get. You can change your mind, your smartness, and who you become.	People have fixed traits, such as smartness, intelligence, and personality, that they cannot change.
Learning takes time and effort, so trying hard is valued.	Learning happens quickly for smart people, so trying hard is not valued; if you have to try hard, you probably aren't smart.
The most important information is *how* someone did (or could do) something, because that's what we can learn from.	The most important information is whether one is successful. It shows who is smart and more valuable. *How* one succeeds is irrelevant. (Cheating and lying can be justifiable routes to success.)
The goal is to learn as much as you can.	The goal is to look as smart as you can.
Frequent success without trying hard indicates choosing activities that are too easy to learn from.	Frequent success without trying is an indicator of one's (fixed) ability and value.
Problems/challenges/errors are to be expected if a person is taking on challenge—which is valued (even experts/authors make mistakes).	Problems/challenges/errors are indicators of one's intellectual ability.
Challenging and novel activities are engaging.	Challenging and novel activities are risky/stressful.
Collaboration is important and success requires it, along with interest and efforts to comprehend. Seeking help is sensible after exhausting one's own resources.	Competition is important and success requires ability and a competitive focus. Seeking help is evidence of one's intellectual inadequacy.
Greater competence means being able to take on new challenges and greater opportunity to help others.	Greater competence means being smarter and therefore better (and more valuable) than others, and potentially having power over others.

*recommended her for chemistry honors and AP Language and
Composition and she maintained a B average in both those classes.*

I am the last person to support high-stakes tests, but their negative effects are maximized when we set up fixed-performance worlds. Of course, the tests themselves drive us toward performance goals by setting up comparisons—school against school, teacher against teacher, student against student—and focusing entirely on a single performance.

Changing Worlds

There is little doubt which is the more productive world view with respect to learning. Indeed, school interventions based on the dynamic-learning framework can change the trajectory of children experiencing difficulty in school.[18] The obvious question is, how do we help children take up a dynamic-learning frame rather than a fixed-performance frame? There are three major points of influence. The first is what we choose to say when children are successful or unsuccessful at something—when we give children feedback or praise. Sometimes the significant language is quite subtle. For example, it turns out to matter whether we say "Good job" or "Good boy."[19] Different forms of feedback nurture different narratives about self. I take this up in Chapter 4.

The second point of influence is the way we frame activities. For example, introducing an activity by saying "Let's see who's the best (or quickest) at doing these problems" is very different from "Let's see which of these problems is the most interesting." These will lead children to different understandings of what they are doing, focus their attention on different information, and turn their energies toward different goals.

A third point of influence is what we explicitly teach children about how people's brains and minds work. For example, if children know that each time they learn something new, their brain literally grows new cells, they can apply that to their thinking about the stability of intelligence.[20] However, before I take up these very practical matters, I want to pursue fixed and dynamic theorizing a little further, because they don't just apply to theories of intelligence, and they don't just apply to students.

Beyond Being Smart

People (and that includes teachers) apply fixed or dynamic theorizing to a range of human characteristics besides intelligence. For example, teachers who agree with the statement "Some people are just not as smart as others and there's not much they can do about it" also tend to agree with the statement "If someone is lazy in one situation, they will be lazy in another situation."[21] If a child doesn't get up to help at clean-up time in the classroom and we hold a fixed theory, we will interpret the behavior as a sign of laziness—a general personal trait expected across situations. From this view, a child's performance on a single test can indicate their intelligence, in any context, now and forever, and their performance on a single writing effort can indicate permanent aptitude for writing poetry. This fixed theorizing about characteristics is institutionalized in some views of teaching. For example, the Teacher Vision website, before offering a list of traits for book reports, notes that "characters (and real-life people) have unique attributes called traits."[22] The list of traits offered includes smart, brave, impulsive, intelligent, lazy, creative, messy, and wild. I view these descriptors and the ways they are introduced as invitations to fixed-performance thinking.

Within a fixed-performance perspective, people can be judged quite quickly. Indeed, people who take up fixed theorizing form stereotypes more quickly than those choosing dynamic theorizing, they are more inclined to apply trait thinking in describing group members, and they make more extreme trait judgments, whether positive or negative.[23] In fact, people choosing fixed theorizing focus on information that confirms their stereotypes, ignoring disconfirming information. The more information goes against their stereotype, such as a poor, low-achieving boy doing well on a test, the less attention they give to that information. Within a fixed theory, once a student is judged as lazy (or friendly or learning disabled, etc.) we start to see evidence of it everywhere in their behavior. Their situation and psychological processes, such as intentions and feelings, take a back seat.

When we take up a dynamic frame, we do the reverse, giving less credibility to stereotype and focusing more on disconfirming or neutral information.[24] As Daniel Molden and Carol Dweck put it, "When people's psychological processes hold special meaning, inconsistent information, rather than being a threat to one's views, may be welcomed as a way of forming a more nuanced view of someone's beliefs, desires, or habits."[25] We will see other reasons for the importance of this stance toward difference in Chapter 6. People adopting a dynamic frame are aware of common stereotypes; they just don't accept them as accurate descriptions of people. They believe that behavior is influenced by the context. Just because a person can solve (or not) one kind of problem in one situation, doesn't mean she can solve (or not) all sorts of problems in all sorts of situations, now and forever. People adopting a dynamic frame can imagine that someone might behave badly because of a particular situation, perhaps being tired or anxious or hungry.

Theories, Relationships, and Feelings

It will come as no surprise that our theories have implications for our relationships with other people. If we judge quickly and stereotype people, it will limit our likely relationships with them. Indeed, when conflicts arise in personal relationships, if we pose the problem in terms of the partner's traits and habitual intentions, the relationship is pretty much doomed. Using the words "You always . . ." or "You never . . ." in a committed relationship is probably the quickest route to celibacy. Within a fixed theory, relationships are a matter of destiny and the permanent characteristics of the participants—things over which we have no control. Since the problem can be traced to fixed traits, they're either mine or yours. When conflicts arise, I can either avoid the problem or become hostile and blaming. By contrast, with a dynamic-learning view of relationships, people view problems as good places for improving the relationship. When they disagree, they adopt strategies that work toward improving the relationship.[26] When people are trying to learn something together and they disagree, dynamic-learning theorists focus on the conflict in ideas and try to integrate their different perspectives. In the process, each develops a more positive view of his or her partner's ability. Not so for fixed-performance theorizers. For them the disagreement represents a threat to their ability. If one person is right, the other must be wrong. They turn the disagreement into a relational conflict. They put their partner down in order to protect their view of their own ability.[27]

People with a dynamic theory expect that people act as they do because of their psychological processes—what they believe, know, and feel. Because of this, when they are wronged by someone else, their tendency is to try to understand and educate the offender and to look for ways to forgive. They expect people to change and to be persuadable. When children are told little vignettes in which a child misbehaves and are asked whether they think the child will behave the same or differently in a couple of weeks, children with dynamic theories expect change. Children with fixed theories judge the child in the vignette and his or her behavior more harshly, expect no change in the behavior, and are more inclined to simply punish rather than educate the offender.[28]

You might think this judging and punishing only applies to adults. Rest assured that it is much the same for children. For example, children who adopt fixed theories evaluate peers who misbehave more negatively than do those who adopt dynamic theories. They expect that the peer will behave just as badly the next time they see him, and their inclination is to punish him.[29] Those who adopt dynamic theories, on the other hand, explain behavior in terms of mental processes—feelings, beliefs, and what people know and don't know. Consequently, these children view and respond to problem behavior differently.

When faced with transgressions, people holding dynamic theories try to understand the thinking and the context of the transgression, to educate and forgive the transgressor. They think the misbehavior is more likely temporary and they are inclined to help make it so. In a classroom, this position leans toward a restorative justice stance—repairing an error rather than simply judging and punishing the perpetrator. This view is consistent with all error in the classroom. When a child makes a spelling error, the idea is to understand what went into the production of the error and to educate.

Fixed and dynamic theories also have implications for our feelings. For example, college students holding a fixed theory are more vulnerable to depressive thinking and allow it to impact their personal and academic work. When things don't go well they begin to criticize themselves about their traits and abilities. They think of themselves as "losers," and this leads to depressive thinking and a spiral downward that also affects their self-esteem. Challenges and depressive feelings affect students holding dynamic theories very differently. They interpret them as reasons to act, and they actually improve their performance after failure. They don't encounter the downward spiral or the consequent loss of self-esteem.[30] This is the case for both teachers and children, and the consequences are important in both cases.

Not only is the dynamic-learning world more interesting academically, it is also more interesting socially. Since learning is fundamentally social, basing a classroom on dynamic-learning principles offers a double boost to learning. For example, middle school students with dynamic-learning theories were more likely than those with fixed-performance theories to have friendship relationships characterized by trust, mutual sharing of difficulties, and adaptive social problem solving.[31] These consequences of the dynamic-learning and fixed-performance frames are summarized in Figure 2.2.

Okay, you ask, how do we make it hard to open the door to the dark side while propping open the door to a better world? I take up this question in the next two chapters.

**Figure 2.2 Consequences of Dynamic-Learning and
Fixed-Performance Frames**

Dynamic-Learning Frame	Fixed-Performance Frame
Explain behaviors in terms of mental processes and context.	Explain behaviors in terms of permanent traits.
Choose challenging activities in which they will learn as much as possible. Get into their zone of proximal development.[32]	Choose activities that make them look smart—easy enough to be successful but not quite difficult enough to make errors and learn.
When encountering difficulty, engage in self-monitoring and self-instruction, increase strategic efforts, and don't see self as failing.	When encountering difficulty, view the difficulty as failure, question their ability, assign blame for failure, and cease acting strategically.
What advice would they give to a peer who is having difficulty? Lots of strategic advice.	Advice offered a peer who is having difficulty would be minimal and perhaps accompanied by sympathy.
Feel smart when taking on challenges or teaching others.	Feel smart when they do it better or faster than others.
What do they make of a new child in class who misbehaves (or does badly on work)? Probably not a bad student; probably better in a couple of weeks.	Probably a bad student; probably much the same in a couple of weeks.
When faced with transgressions, try to understand the thinking and the context that produced the behavior, and forgive and educate the transgressor.	When faced with transgressions, invoke punishment.
When faced with disagreements in the process of learning: engage the disagreement and try to synthesize the views. Enhance view of partner in the process.	Turn the disagreement into a relational confrontation. Put partner down.
Are slow to judge and form stereotypes.	Judge quickly and form stereotypes.
Older students think education is to help people understand the world and to prepare them for socially useful work.	Older students think the purpose of education is to enhance wealth and socioeconomic status.

CHAPTER 3

Changing Learning Narratives

It's not that I'm so smart, it's just that I stay with problems longer.
—ALBERT EINSTEIN[1]

Children, like the rest of us, are constantly making sense of their world, and the same world can look entirely different from one person to the next—or for the same person from one moment to the next. The world is perceptually ambiguous. Take the classic illustration in Figure 3.1, for example.[2] You might see a young woman or an old woman. By pointing out that the long facial feature can be either a nose or a cheek, or that the neckband can also be a mouth, I might destabilize the image for you. That is what we do when we try to help children take up a dynamic-learning frame; we point out to them those features of the world that draw attention to the frame. By promoting any of the beliefs

Figure 3.1

25

underlying the dynamic-learning network, we can simultaneously limit the likelihood of children seeing the world through a fixed-performance frame. We try to do this at every opportunity, and we get the most mileage out of turning their attention to change rather than stability, and process more than performance, and by changing the way they think about error.

Change and Stability

Martin's Big Words by Doreen Rappaport is a wonderful illustrated book about Martin Luther King Jr. Pegeen Jensen is about to read it to her first-grade students when one of them points out that their kindergarten teacher read it to them. Other students agree. Here's how she responds to them:

> **Pegeen:** This is not a really long book but it has got really big ideas inside of it. So it's important to read it every year I think. Because are you the same person, exactly the same person you were in kindergarten?
> **Students:** No.
> **Pegeen:** No, I hope not. What has grown besides your body? What's grown and changed besides your body?
> **Students:** Your brain.
> **Pegeen:** Your brain. So when you hear these words, this time you might think differently about this book.[3]

Your brain is changing and so is the way you experience ideas. Expect to change.

Turning attention to change rather than stability makes a difference to all kinds of learning. For example, people can learn to raise or lower their heart rate.[4] If you first direct them to monitor the variability in their heart rate, it is subsequently easier for them to gain control of it. If, instead, you direct them to monitor the stability of their heart rate, it is subsequently harder for them to exercise control of it.

The thread of change and growth is woven firmly into the conversational fabric of Pegeen's classroom. The thread will not be repeated the same way next time and it won't have to be explained in as much detail, but it will routinely show up. For example, Pegeen's students have constructed time lines of their lives, replete with photos and annotations, and posted them on the wall, inviting conversations about change. And as they begin a unit on writing memoir, Pegeen asks, "Patricia Polacco writes what kind of stories?" and the children, because they have already talked about this, answer, "Memoir."

"Memoir," she repeats. "What makes it a memoir?"

"It's about their lives," Sam observes.

Alexis adds, "It's a special story from our lives."

Tim extends it further, "And maybe when she looks back at it and thinks about its importance . . . Sometimes it's hard to think about how you might change a little bit because of that experience."

Pegeen turns their attention to Tim's observation about change. "Did you hear what Tim said?" Foregrounding their careful listening to each other, she asks, "Stephen, would you repeat what he said for us so we can think about it?"

Stephen summarizes, "It's when you look back and you learn how much you've grown and changed."

Deciding which things in life are essentially fixed, beyond our power to change, and which things we can change (even if it's just a tiny bit) is a constant tension for us. This is the tension between structure and agency. For us to have agency we have to believe that things are changeable, because if they can't be changed, taking action is futile. Children must experience many things as at least potentially changeable, not just aspects of the world outside them, but also aspects of themselves—their learning, their identities, their intellect, their personal attributes, and their ways of relating to others. In the talk of the classroom, we want to hear the threads of a dynamic view of intellect—indeed, of self. We want to inoculate the children against infection by fixed theories; we want them to say "I'm not good at this *yet*" and to take steps to change that. Indeed, *yet* is a key word that we should regularly encourage children to add to their narratives.

Pegeen starts this process at the beginning of the year. When she is showing her first graders the computer room on the second day of school, she says, "This is where you'll be doing things like typing stories, which is really hard, but you'll be able to do it by the end of the year." On the third day she says, "Think how much more we got done by ten o'clock than we did yesterday." They are walking back from the library and nothing is happening. But she observes, "One more hallway. We're building our stamina."

The thread of change runs throughout the year. Near the end of the year, the kindergarten students come to visit the first-grade room to see what it's like and to dispel any anxieties. When they leave, Pegeen reminds her first graders how far they have come. She says now that they have learned so much, perhaps they can help her figure out what she needs to teach the kindergartners about reading when they arrive next year. She writes their suggestions on chart paper. One suggestion is "You can use the pictures to help figure out words."

Pegeen writes down the suggestion, then says, "What if there are no pictures?"

A student responds, "You can make a picture in your mind."

Pegeen repeats the suggestion with expression as she writes it down, "Make a picture in your mind." She then asks, "How many of you do that? Karla, your hand went up really quickly. Would you have done that back in March?" Karla and all the other students are again reminded, with evidence, that you get smarter the more you learn. At the same time, Pegeen has spent some valuable time reviewing strategies, assessing her students' understandings, and affirming them as knowledgeable people. In Pegeen's class, the conversational current pushes strongly toward the idea that change, particularly in learning, is normal.

Other teachers do this too. Kindergarten teacher Susie Althof comments to her students, "I have to tell you what the first graders are learning about." She gives a brief explanation and then says, "You haven't learned about that yet, but you will." She notes about their use of center time, "You've changed so much this week in how you're doing this." Later she adds, "Wow! You've learned so much since September, haven't you?"

Jeralyn Johnson, a fourth-grade teacher, having spent half an hour teaching her students how to use protractors, observes, "This is our first day of using protractors."

A student offers a judgment on the performance: "And we did good."

Jeralyn takes the student's comment and weaves it into the longer-term change narrative: "We feel better than we did fifteen minutes ago. But by next week we are going to be pros." She affirms that learning takes time and work, but intellectual change happens. The more you learn, the smarter you get.

Change is expected in areas beyond intellect too, as children begin to reimagine themselves and their futures. One of the students in Pegeen's class wrote that Kevin Henke's book *Lilly's Big Day* was her favorite because "Lilly is just a changing person like me!"[5] This link to characters in books is not to be ignored either. If we are going to resist searching for fixed "character traits" in the classroom, we probably shouldn't search for them in the literature the children encounter in school. Rather, in discussions of books we should cast characters not in terms of stable character traits, but in terms of internal states, feelings, intentions, contexts, and change. During one book discussion in Pegeen's classroom, for example, a child commented about a character, "He's a bad boy."

Pegeen immediately observed, "He just made a bad choice, don't you think?" In this classroom, nobody is going to be a bad person. They will however, make bad decisions, and those bad decisions do not imply that the person is bad. These conversations are consistent, regardless of who is being talked about.

In her kindergarten classroom, Susie was explaining to me that someone had broken into the classroom and taken the document camera. One of the children excitedly jumped in with, "Yeah, the bad guy broke the window and . . ." Susie immediately reframed the narrative. "Not a bad guy. He just made a decision for his own benefit and didn't consider other people." Making decisions in which you consider others' perspectives is a consistent classroom conversational thread—along with taking control of and deliberately changing your life by making choices. Front and center, though, is the fact that people are not permanently good or bad. Different situations, more learning, and different decisions all can change a person.

Stability and the Meaning of Error

The expectation of change is very important, but in order to manage the idea of constant change, children also need to have a sense of stability, a sense of what they can count on. In productive classrooms there are routines and rituals that give a sense of stability and control. We have plans for the day, possibly with input from the children, and we regularly remind them of where we are in the schedule so that they can predict what's next and how best to use their time. This is not to say that we don't change the schedule, but it will be cause for discussion if we do. If children can't count on having a regular time to write, or on civil order in the classroom, they can't easily deal with ongoing change. However, they must also be able to count on respect and freedom from personal judgment. If their self-worth, rather than being constant, is contingent on whether or not they are successful, then they will not be able to manage change well. So we make it clear that we (and the other students) care for and respect them—even when they are unsuccessful or make less than optimal decisions. Our respect is such that we assume that children will try to fix their error and make better decisions next time. We make it clear that we assume it in our talk and we make opportunities to clarify the matter in class meetings and the like.

For example, in a class meeting shortly after Barack Obama's 2009 presidential election, one of Susie Althof's African American kindergarten students brought up the fact that she saw Obama on the television and that he's the president. A brief discussion began, to which Susie added, "Do you think that when Barack Obama was a young boy in kindergarten, do think that sometimes he made mistakes?" There is broad agreement from the students. Susie responds, "And so what did he do to solve that?"

There is a clamor of "Fix it!"

Susie observes, "That's exactly right. And it's okay to make mistakes, and as you start fixing your mistakes or figuring out what you believe as a person and how you're going to treat each other as you grow older you can become that kind of person, right?"

Teachers like Susie also make it clear that they are interested in children—their lives, their concerns, and their interests—so they listen carefully to students whenever they get a chance and make it clear that they listened by referring later to what they heard. For example, "Dequan, you go downtown a lot don't you?" and "Tashia, is that how it is with your baby brother?" They also take children's decisions and choices seriously. I was struck by Susie's response to a kindergarten student who was not fully attending in the small-group Big Book lesson. She asked, quite genuinely, "Do you want to attend to this book or do you want to read by yourself?"

The student responded, "Read by myself."

Without batting an eye, and without judgment, Susie said, "Okay. Off you go." And, he did. He sat down by himself in one of the book corners and read, occasionally looking up and spending a little time listening to the group lesson. Later Susie asked him how it went for him and tried to learn why the group work was not engaging for him in this instance. While establishing a sense of respect, Susie was also establishing for the child a sense of autonomy, which is related to well-being, performance, creativity, and the quality of personal relationships.[6]

Children's job responsibilities are another point of stability in the classroom because they give a useful identity anchor, so we promote the idea that job responsibilities are personally important. We need to have responsibilities to feel accomplished. For example, in Susie's kindergarten class, children have responsibilities, including being the teacher for certain routines. On one occasion, Susie realized she had just taken the responsibility of reviewing the class schedule to organize for the next part of class. She immediately apologized, "I'm sorry, Shatara. I just did your job." With a single utterance, she apologized, reviewed the normality of making errors (and of apologizing when they are social ones), and implicitly recognized that Shatara (as everyone else) is a person who takes her responsibilities seriously. These are all small events, but they add up to the children understanding that they are valued, and they will be even when they make mistakes. Because we all make mistakes, even teachers and presidents, and it doesn't make us bad people. It makes us people who are trying—taking on challenges in order to learn. This is the central anchor that allows children to handle difficulties and change.

Problem Solving and Causal Processes

The strongest thread in the warp of the dynamic-learning fabric is attention to processes, particularly causal processes: observations of the form "You did this, so this happened" or "This happened because you did this." For example, you might say, "Look how you figured that out together. You made a plan, you listened to each other, you made a diagram . . . I don't think you would have figured it out without doing that." Causal process comments are the most effective way of promoting the belief that the important information is how someone did (or could do) something, because that's what we can learn from. Observing or experiencing success (or not) is only usefully instructive when we see how it was accomplished. Process information is particularly effective at undermining the belief that success shows who is smart. Process information removes the "genius" from performance and replaces it with both a dynamic-learning frame and the strategic knowledge of how the success was accomplished.

The simplest way into process conversations is to ask how questions: "How did you do that?" "How did you know that?" These questions encourage children to rehearse agentive narratives—to explain how they had an effect on the world. At the same time, children make their strategies available to the rest of the learning community. Most important, they invite dynamic-learning theories and undermine fixed-performance theories.

For example, Susie has just been reading a Big Book with her kindergarten students, during which she drew their attention to the use of pictures to figure out words, mostly by asking "How could we figure that out?" and then revoicing their words in clearer terms: "Oh, so if we look at the picture we can tell which word makes sense." Then, rather than praising them, she offers a comment that positions them power-fully: "Thanks for teaching us that." Next, she offers them a choice of books for their independent reading. They choose their books and head off to their reading spots. As they leave to do their independent or interdependent reading she says, "I can't wait to see how you look at the pictures and figure it out." As she checks in with different students, she can be heard again turning their attention to the process, saying, "How did you figure out that word was *monster* and not *troll*?" and "Ask your partner how he did it." This latter invitation is an explicit attempt to build process-oriented conversations among peers, and thus to expand the amount of teaching that occurs without the teacher. As a follow-up on the strategies they have been revealing, she adds, referring to the hero in a Big Book they've been reading, "Doesn't it feel like you have all that power—like Dan the Flying Man—power to figure out how to write those words?"

Asking children "How did you do that?" gives them a reason to retrace their steps in accomplishing something, such as solving a math problem, writing a poem, or cleaning up after an art project or science experiment. This narrative makes what might have been a series of unplanned and unconscious steps into a packaged strategy linked to a goal—a strategic action that can later be invoked for planning and refining. However, much of the intellectual process actually takes place inside our heads, and making current mental processes available to our-selves and others requires that we articulate them. Articulating these mental processes is most useful when they are still in process and can be capitalized on for assessment purposes and revised so they are most pro-ductive. Asking "What are you thinking?" is a simple way to expand this process thread in classroom talk.

These "How did you . . ." and "What are you thinking?" conversa-tions invite agentive narratives, increase the available strategic informa-tion, reduce the likelihood of fixed-performance theories, and, at the same time, invite dynamic-learning theories. It is not surprising, then, that children with dynamic theories, if asked, are prepared to give their peers specific suggestions for how to do better. Henry's classroom is just such an environment, and when asked what advice he might give to a classmate about how to become a better reader, he observes, "If they are reading harder books that are too hard for them, [tell them] not to push themselves as much . . . maybe later in a couple of months read those books. Push them to the side and read, like, books that are at your level."[7] By contrast, children with fixed theories are much less likely to offer suggestions. What can you say to help someone whose problem is permanent?[8] This availability of advice for peers is one component of building the children's ability to teach. Even in kindergarten, children are learning to teach—a topic I will take up in Chapter 8.

Before her students head off to begin writing, a teacher asks, "Are you ready to get started? Do you have a plan? You don't need to tell me your plan. I might be able to figure out what your plan is from your behavior." In the process, she makes it clear that planning is expected and invites children to rehearse a process narrative in advance—a practice that not only makes the class run more smoothly but also promotes optimism. Yes, optimism. Ellen Langer and her colleagues gave undergraduates an apparently hopeless scenario and asked them to rate the likelihood that they could accomplish a goal.[9] They were to imagine scenarios such as being at a party and seeing a very attractive person with whom they would like to get a date. Unfortunately, they had the flu and a very serious outbreak of acne, and they had spilled ketchup on their clothes.[10] The students then rated their chances of getting the date and they were very pessimistic. A comparison group, before rating their chances, was asked to think of ways they might achieve their goal. When they subsequently rated their chances, this group was quite optimistic. The more process options people have at the disposal of their imagination, the better. There are plenty of reasons to be interested in optimism, but here's one: optimism reduces the risk of death from heart attack.[11]

The focus on problem solving and causal processes should be taken up at every turn. For example, in discussing a book with the children, rather than focusing on the protagonist's character traits, Pegeen draws attention to his problem solving—the causal process link—since that is the heart of the narrative she would like them to take up:

> **Pegeen:** Think about Micodo. He's coming from Japan; he's
>   coming to a new country; what do you think his problem is?
> **Marco:** Same thing happened with me.
> **Pegeen:** I bet you're understanding how Micodo feels. What do
>   you think his problem is?
> **Marco:** Leaving, leaving your good friends and that stuff
> **Pegeen:** Oh, leaving your good friends, so you—Dan, go ahead.
> **Dan:** He might not make as much friends as he thinks.
> **Pegeen:** He might be nervous about making friends . . . How
>   does he solve that problem of being nervous and maybe not
>   making any new friends?

In this book discussion, Pegeen's conversations are consistent with the classroom dynamic-learning conversational threads. People, she points out, are affected by the contexts in which they live. They encounter problems, have feelings, and take actions to solve the problems. It is not just academics that require such thinking. Social problems are also amenable to change through strategic thinking. At the same time, she turns Marco's and Dan's comments into mind-reading observations, and by taking their contributions seriously, she shows the respect that is their anchor as they take on challenge.

These conversational threads consistently invoke a dynamic-learning frame and disrupt the fixed-performance frame. We will explore many other ways to establish the dynamic-learning frame, some easier than others, in other chapters. How we give children feedback is probably the most difficult for us to change, but it is probably the point of most leverage. We will take up this challenge in the next chapter.

CHAPTER 4

"Good Job!" Feedback, Praise, and Other Responses

The trouble with most of us is that we would rather be ruined by praise than saved by criticism.

—Norman Vincent Peale[1]

If you need encouragement, praise, pats on the back from everybody, then you make everybody your judge.

—Unknown[2]

Jeralyn's fourth graders are going to vote on which book gets the classroom book award for the year. They take turns standing and speaking for their favorite, trying hard to persuade others to vote for their choice. After a student makes a pitch, other students are moved by and celebrate the words chosen and the performance of the book review. Feedback the students volunteer includes these statements:

"He used strong language."
"He got right to the point."
"It's the way he said it. It moves you."
"He gets to your heart."

This feedback is not given by the teacher, but it is surely grounded in the kind of feedback the teacher gives. It is still early in the year, but the students' observations focus attention on specific features of the performances. Their feedback will become even more focused and productive as the year goes on.

In kindergarten, Tatiana has figured out how to write a difficult word with invented spelling. She takes it to her teacher. Her teacher does not say "Good girl" or "Nice job," which would be common responses in other classrooms. Instead, she asks, "How did you do that?"—a response that prompts Tatiana to tell the story of her efforts. In the process, she rehearses a narrative in which she acts and makes choices that have desired consequences—an agentive narrative that indentifies her as a person who accomplishes things by acting strategically. Her teacher then suggests with enthusiasm, "You should go and tell Antoine."

Tatiana does, and Antoine says, "How did you do it?" which prompts her to rehearse the agentive narrative again and share the strategy with Antoine. In this chapter, I explore what we know about interactions like these among teachers and students, and the consequences of different forms of feedback. I chose the particular examples in this chapter to emphasize the fact that much of the feedback children experience comes from their peers. We have to remember that we are not just giving students feedback; we are also teaching them to provide it. In a way, we are teaching them to teach. If students can provide productive feedback, then collectively they will tend to get more feedback. And it will be more immediate feedback, because, rather than waiting for the teacher, their peers can provide it. More feedback improves learning, and immediate feedback is more effective than delayed feedback.[3] Increasing the responsiveness of the classroom by actively teaching students how to respond to each other's efforts magnifies the effects of our teaching. It increases the intensity of classroom instruction and changes the social genetics of the next generation of parents and teachers.

Process Versus Person Feedback

There have been many studies of the effects of feedback on students' behavior. Consider a study by Melissa Kamins and Carol Dweck in which kindergarten children role-play with toy dolls four different failure experiences.[4] The experiences are mild, such as failing to stack blocks away neatly or unsuccessfully cleaning up after snack time. The teacher responds to each role-play event by saying either "The blocks are all crooked and in one big mess; *I'm very disappointed in you*" or "The blocks are all crooked and in one big mess; *maybe you should find another way to do it*." After four of these identical failure-feedback role-play events, there is a failure event with neutral feedback: "That house [you built with Legos] has no windows." In other words, some children had four role-play experiences of person-oriented criticism (*I'm disappointed in you*) and others had four experiences of process-oriented criticism (*maybe you should find another way to do it*). All had a final neutral-feed-back experience.

The children were then asked to rate their final neutral role-play experience. How did they like their house without windows? The process-feedback group, on average, gave their imperfect house almost 3.8 out of 5 points. How did they feel about the whole experience? Quite good. Did it make them feel smart? It did. Did it make them feel good? Yes, it did. How would they finish the story about the house with no windows? They pose solutions like: "I can do it again better if I take my time," "I'd make another building with windows," and "I would say it's not finished yet, then I could cut out squares from paper and paste them onto the house."[5] Notice that these students' responses are consistent with the feedback. "Maybe you should find another way to do it" makes the error temporary and points to an agentive solution—fix it.

The children who were told in the role-play that they were disappointing had a very different experience. They gave their house 2.2 out of 5 (a standard deviation less than the process group). They didn't feel good about the experience, they didn't feel smart, and they couldn't come up with a constructive resolution to the story. Instead, they role-played crying and other helpless behavior, generating comments such as "She should cry and go to bed," "The teacher got mad and went home," "My sister saw and got real upset that there were no windows," and "He should get a time out."[6] In other words, the feedback teaches the children the meaning of error and affects whether or not children are likely to persist.

The moral of the story might be: Don't use person-oriented criticism like "I'm disappointed in you" or "You're not good at this" or "You're a bad boy." These lead children into debilitating fixed-performance worlds. If you're going to offer critique, focus on the process and possibility.

I doubt that readers of this book would regularly use person-oriented criticism. However, the researchers repeated the study using success experiences and five different forms of *praise*. The children in each group had four success experiences followed by one of the following comments:

Group 1: You're a good boy.

Group 2: I'm proud of you.

Group 3: You're very good at this.

Group 4: You tried really hard.

Group 5: You found a good way to do it; could you think of other ways that would also work?

After the four successes, the child dolls encountered a failure experience, again with neutral feedback: "The bus [you drew] has no wheels." It turns out that the first three forms of praise—"You're a good boy," "I'm proud of you," and "You're very good at this"—produce the same effects as the person-oriented criticism. In other words, saying "I'm proud of you" has the same effect as saying "I'm disappointed in you." It's just the other end of the same conversation. We only have to mark one end of the proud/disappointed conversation for the children to be pulled into that conversation. If we say "I'm proud of you" when they're successful, they will fill in the other end of the conversation and infer our disappointment when they are unsuccessful. We don't have to say anything. They are learning that, in this domain, we judge people.

The last two forms of feedback, "You tried really hard" and "You found a good way to do it; could you think of other ways that would also work?" focus on different aspects of the process—effort and strategy—and not on the person. Both resulted in children feeling good about themselves and their work, feeling capable, and being able to find productive enactments to solve the problem of the mistake. The moral of the story: Don't use person-oriented praise. Instead, use process-oriented feedback.

There is one last important piece to this research that relates to moral development, which we will return to in Chapter 8. The children were asked to imagine a new student in class who "steals your crayons, scribbles on your paper and spills your juice. Then she [he] calls you names."[7] They were asked whether they expected the new student to continue to act this way. The process-oriented students viewed the bad behavior as potentially changeable. The person-oriented students saw the behavior as permanent. The students were also told of an imaginary new student who makes many mistakes on his schoolwork, and were asked whether that means the student is bad. The process-feedback students felt the mistakes did not indicate badness. The children who had received the person-oriented feedback, however, felt that, yes, he was a bad student. The person-oriented feedback had drawn students into a fixed-performance world. Another way to think about it is that, when we make personal judgments of children, whether through praise or criticism, we teach them to do the same. They learn to judge themselves and others. They develop a sense of contingent self-worth—that they are only able, good, and worthy when they are successful.

The children who had the process or effort feedback were not affected in the same way. They did not think their imaginary peer was bad and thought it unlikely he would always behave that way. They adopted a dynamic-learning frame and expected change.

Small Differences in Language

Surprisingly small changes in feedback can have quite broad consequences, because the feedback marks whether we are in the fixed-performance world or the dynamic-learning world. Let me give you another example. Using role-play in a similar way to the studies I have already described, only with puppets, Andrei Cimpian and his colleagues, working with four- to five-year-olds, compared the effects of saying "You are a good drawer" and "You did a good job drawing."[8] As with the other studies, this one began with four successful events in which a teacher puppet asked the child's puppet to draw imaginary objects using a pipe cleaner as a pretend pencil. With each event, half the children were told "You are a good drawer," and the other half "You did a good job drawing." The children were then asked to rate how much they liked their drawing, whether the event made them feel happy or sad, whether it made them feel like they were good at drawing, and whether it made them feel like a good boy or girl. There were no differences between the groups after these successful experiences.

Next the children role-played two mistake scenarios. The teacher pointed out the mistakes to both groups with the same neutral feedback, "The cat has no ears" and "The bus has no wheels." Now, after experiencing failure, the children were asked the same four questions—how much they liked their drawing, whether what happened made them feel happy or sad, good or bad at drawing, and a good or bad girl or boy. In each case, the children who initially received the person-oriented praise, "You are a good drawer," responded less positively. The slightly different, but more process-oriented "You did a good job drawing" produced more positive responses in the children. The difference was particularly marked in the question regarding whether they felt happy or sad.

But the researchers didn't stop there. They asked the children to choose which drawing they might try again on another day, and whether, given a choice, they would choose to draw or to do something else. Those who received the person-oriented praise were less likely to choose to draw next time if they had a choice, and if they had to draw they would choose a picture they were already successful at. Process feedback led to more interest in drawing, and to an interest in taking up challenge.

Finally, the children were reminded of each error story in turn, and asked, "What would you do now?" The researchers were again interested in which children would have their puppet adopt a constructive solution strategy, such as "Fix it." The children who had received person-oriented praise were less able to generate a solution, preferring to "walk away," or, as one child said, "Cry. I would do it for both of them. Yeah, for the wheels and the ears."[9]

In other words, feedback that helps children think that their performance reveals some permanent quality, intelligence, or goodness at drawing (or anything else), has some serious side effects. These side effects include enjoying the activities less, being less resilient in the face of difficulty, being less likely to choose the activity on another occasion, being more likely to judge themselves and others, and generating unproductive narratives to explain their experience. These, in turn, have other consequences. For example, the narrative styles we develop for explaining events affect the likelihood that we will experience depression.[10]

What I find striking about these studies is that only a few instances of a particular form of feedback produce quite strong effects. We have to imagine the consequences of these patterns magnified over the days, weeks, months, and years children spend in school. We also have to consider the extent of the effects. The effects are on children's thinking, their emotions, their resilience when they are unsuccessful, and their relationships with others.

Clearly, process- and effort-oriented feedback are the best options—indeed, effort is a part of the process. Trying is more important than success. Although effort and process feedback have had equivalent effects in these studies, I am inclined to go with process feedback where possible. First, it gets children into the habit of explaining successes and failures in terms of strategy use. This explanation is less risky than effort explanations, because often effort simply isn't enough. Besides, a student may already be working as hard as she can, or have not worked hard at all. Second, the more process talk becomes part of classroom conversations, the more strategy instruction will be occurring incidentally, without the teacher having to do it. Adding "Could you think of other ways that would also work?" is even better, because it invites children to imagine alternative strategies, building flexibility. They learn that when one strategy doesn't work, there are probably other ways to get things done.

Criticism of Praise

It is common wisdom in the United States that we should lavish praise upon children, particularly those who aren't as successful as others, in order to build their self-esteem. I found an example on the Read Write Inc. website (a phonics program) in their letter to parents.[11] The letter offers this advice: "Please remember that children learn more rapidly if they are constantly praised," "Always praise your child," "This is difficult for many children so be lavish with your praise!" I hope I have already made you a bit cautious about this advice. At least if you are going to praise, you will need to think about what kind of praise to offer. However, I'd like to suggest some further cautions about praise.

To begin with, public praise carries a real risk, as we see in the cartoon in Figure 4.1.

Whenever we publicly say "good" to one student and then follow it with "excellent" to another, suddenly "good" isn't worth as much.

Figure 4.1

IT'S ALWAYS 'GOOD DOG'— NEVER 'GREAT DOG.'

GREGORY

Worse, it can become "damning with faint praise." But even private praise has complexities. When children are fully engaged in an activity, if we praise them we can simply distract them from what they were doing and turn their attention to pleasing us. Even process-oriented praise can do this. For example, often we begin our feedback with "I like the way you . . .," which ensures that we turn attention to a process. As we know, turning attention to the process invites a process-oriented, agentive narrative to explain successes and failures. It turns attention away from fixed explanations. The "I like . . ." part is not as helpful. Rather than offering an agentive narrative, it offers a judgment and implies that the point of the child's efforts is to please you. Let's consider some alternatives.

Alternatives to Praise

What if instead we said, "Look at how you . . ." That would simply turn children's attention to the process and away from fixed-theory explanations.[12] An even better alternative would be, for example, "When you added dialogue to your piece, I really understood how Amy [the character] felt." This is not so much praise as a causal statement—you did this [added dialogue], with this consequence [I understood how the character felt]. Causal process statements are at the heart of building agency. They show the consequence of a process, making it into a tool that the child can use again on another occasion to accomplish a similar end. Consider the following interaction around a kindergartner's picture, from the excellent book *Talking, Drawing, Writing: Lessons for Our Youngest Writers* by Martha Horn and Mary Ellen Giacobbe.[13] On the day before the following exchange, the children discussed how writers revise by asking themselves questions such as "What do I need to add [or change] so readers will understand my story?" Janaya has agreed to show her book to the class. The teacher invites Janaya to tell her story, and after she does, the teacher begins with this observation:

> **Teacher:** And yesterday, when Janaya went back to work, this is what was on the page: there was the picture of you, over here, and the picture of your dad, here, and your friend's house, here, right? And then Janaya added some other parts. [Pointing to the yellow car] You added this, didn't you? Tell us about this.
> **Janaya:** That's my dad's car when he came to pick me up.

Teacher: Oh, so your mom dropped you off at your friend's house.

Janaya: [Pointing to the blue car] That's my mom's car. She's leaving to go to work.

Teacher: Oh, so here's your mom's car—you added that, too—and she dropped you off and she's driving to work? [Janaya nods.] And I see you added this part, where your dad is standing. Tell us about this.

Janaya: It's the thing where you walk.

Teacher: Oh, the sidewalk? I can see the lines, just the way they look in the sidewalk. So he got out of the car to get you and he's standing on the sidewalk! [Janaya nods.]

Teacher: Boys and girls, we can tell where this story is happening, can't we? We see the sidewalk, the flower, the outside of the house, and the cars, so we know the story takes place outside. And we know something about the people, don't we? We know this is Janaya and this is her dad. You know, Janaya, before you even told us who these people were, I just knew this was you! [Addressing the other students.] You know how I could tell?

Students: She's small and that one's big! / She has a dress!

Teacher: Well, yes, it seems that this would be Janaya because she is small and this would be her dad because he's bigger, but also, I could tell because of the hair. You made your hair look just the way you wear it, with a ponytail like that. And I'll bet your dad's hair is like this? [Janaya nods.] And you made yourself small and your dad big, so we could guess that this was a little person who was with a big person, like a kid with a mom or dad.

Teacher: [Looking at the children on the rug.] You know what I think? I think Janaya wanted her readers to understand her story about her mom dropping her off and her playing outside and her dad coming to pick her up in his car. She added information to help readers understand: She made people's hair the way it looks, she made people dressed the way they dress, and she made it look like it was happening outside because we can see the outside of the house and the cars and the flower.

Janaya, I notice that you didn't color the faces of the people. Don't forget that in the caddies we have these different shades of skin color so you can make the skin of the people look real.

Although there is no praise here, the child leaves the interaction feeling positive, confident, and motivated. There are several important reasons. First, the teacher shows the effectiveness of the illustrator's choices in informing her audience. Second, the teacher's observations position Janaya as a writer-illustrator who makes intentional and consequential decisions, showing her respect by taking the work seriously. Third, by not judging it as good or otherwise, the teacher shows that judging is not what happens in this class. Instead, we think about how and why people do things. By not judging, the teacher also positions herself beside rather than above the student, avoiding an asymmetrical power relationship, the importance of which we'll get to later (indeed, the teacher is sitting down with the child standing next to her, with faces at similar heights). Fourth, the teacher rehearses over and over the causal/intentional narrative: Janaya did *x*, so we understand better. The seeds of this narrative are in the setup from the previous day: "What do I need to add [or change] so readers will understand my story?" Fifth, the teacher invites Janaya (and the others who are listening) to try yet another intentional strategy, coloring the faces to make them more real.

In one classroom, I watched a first grader using the pointer to point to the words on a Big Book while the other children read them. He was concentrating very hard. When he finished he went to sit down, and I expected his teacher to say "Good boy" or "Good job," but she simply said, "Thank you, Ramon." He straightened his shoulders just as much with the thank-you as with any praise, but the thank-you, by not offering judgment, and by recognizing that help was provided, did not create the asymmetrical power relationship that praise might have created. Indeed, the thank-you defined the activity he was engaged in as contributing to the group. "Good boy" would have defined the activity for Ramon and for others as a performance, with the teacher in the powerful position of judging. It would have invited the class into the fixed-performance world.

Praise is related to power and control. The more important the person offering praise, the more powerful it is. Praise is also related to insecurity. The more secure a person is in what he is doing, the less impact praise can have. If someone praises you for your ability with basic math facts, chances are you could care less. If they praise you for something about which you harbor some insecurity ("You're a great teacher/writer/singer/artist"), there's a good chance you will take the praise and feel good about it. For the moment, it feels great. Long-term, however, because of the fixed frame it invites, there can be other consequences. At the very least, you know people are judging you.

Praise and Being Positive

Thankfully, most teachers are very positive people, and empathic, too. We like to help children think positively about the world, themselves, and others. When children do not feel positively about themselves, we feel it and try to fix it. Many of us feel uncomfortable for students when they struggle, particularly those we view as less capable, so we have trouble giving them the time they need to struggle successfully. We rush to praise them in order to build their self-esteem and keep them feeling positive about themselves. They quickly take over initiating this pattern. In the following transcript, Samson, a high school student who is in special education, tries hard to give up control of his reading to his tutor, Erin. He keeps inviting her to either make decisions for him or give him praise. She, however, resists his efforts, insisting that he take control and that he read for himself and not for her.[14]

Speaker	Speech	Analysis
Erin	Ok. Hold up. Here you read 'The blue truck just pulled us.'	Rather than pointing out the error, the teacher offers the student the opportunity to detect it.
Samson	No, that doesn't sound right. I don't know what I got wrong. Isn't this 'just'?	The student makes a brief attempt to solve the problem then invites the teacher to solve it.
Erin	What do you think?	The teacher declines the invitation.
Samson	Yeah.	The student correctly answers his own question.
Erin	Ok, so think about what is happening and try that sentence again. Don't forget to look through the word so you're not just looking at that first letter but you're making sure all the letters match the word you're saying.	Rather than praising what the student has done, the teacher offers a strategy.
Samson	(reading) The blue truck just /p/ /a/ passed us. The blue truck just passed us. Right?	The student applies the strategy, successfully solving the problem and invites the teacher to monitor and praise.

(continued)

Erin	Does it make sense with the story and do the letters match?	The teacher declines the invitation but offers criteria the student can use to monitor himself.
Samson	Uh huh.	The student monitors accurately.
Erin	Ok, so keep moving.	The teacher focuses on maintaining momentum and student control, so does not offer praise.

We tend to think that being positive means praising, but this interaction seems positive in spite of the lack of praise. Samson, in working with Erin, became increasingly engaged in his reading. What counts as positive depends in part on the relationship and in part on the frame of reference. Let me give you another example. A common rule of thumb that has developed in writing circles is to provide at least two positive pieces of feedback for every criticism. It is easy to see why this might be seen as a useful heuristic within a fixed-performance framework. We would be trying to bolster the child's self-esteem before presumably bruising it with the critique. As we have seen, within a fixed-performance framework, feedback that points out confusions or unsuccessful strategies can easily be interpreted as personal criticism. Within a fixed-performance frame, being wrong is an indictment of one's intellect. In a dynamic-learning frame, however, the student's goal is learning and taking on the necessary challenge to do so. When students adopt learning goals, critique of the product, such as "There are no windows on that house," doesn't diminish motivation or personal satisfaction at all. It prompts efforts to fix the problem. It doesn't prompt defensiveness both because the critique is not personal and because it offers an opportunity to learn. In a dynamic-learning frame, receiving help to find and solve a problem is not a negative event. In this framework, self-esteem might not be something you have more or less of either. Perhaps self-esteem is, as Carol Dweck puts it, "a way of experiencing yourself when you are using your resources well."[15]

Critical feedback need not be negative for another reason too—if the "negative" is framed as a potential positive. For example, after responding to a piece of writing, showing that you are taking the writing and the writer seriously, you might offer a potential causal process. This would be structured as follows: "[You did this] and if you [tried this], then [it would have this effect]." This structure offers a direction for development but is less easily construed as negative. The following is an example of this sort of feedback, cast in a language of possibility rather than criticism:

> *The verbs you chose, like* trickled, floated, *and* wafted, *really gave me a sense of the gentle meandering you were trying for in your poem. Have you thought about arranging the poem on the page in a way that might emphasize the meandering even further—like the poets in Paul Janeczko's* A Poke in the I?[16]

This shows the student that you take both her and her writing seriously. It shows a causal process (you chose these verbs, with this effect). Then it gives the student a new possibility to build on what she already has, a place to explore how to do it, a choice to make about whether to do it (another possibility for agency), and a motive for doing so. This next piece of writing feedback has a similar form:

> *You read your piece to the class with such expression that I couldn't help but become interested in wolves. You obviously care about your subject. I also noticed that there were a couple of places in which you lost your expression. Can you remember where they were? [The student points to the places.] You know, writers often read their work out loud like that so they can figure out how to make it better. I wonder whether you could try a couple of different ways to write those sentences and read them out loud a few times to see if you can figure out how to make them flow as well as the rest of the piece. What do you think?*

I hope you see that reducing praise does not mean giving up being positive. It is important to be positive—and particularly important not to be negative. Positive feedback is not really for establishing self-esteem. It is particularly for establishing the foundation on which to build. This is why it is most effective within the zone of proximal development, where it will focus on what Marie Clay called the "partially correct." In other words, positive feedback would show which part of a not quite successful strategy was productive. This has two advantages. First, it takes what the child has already done and turns it into a successful agentive experience. Second, rather than starting from scratch, it starts instruction with something the child already knows.

Mary Ann Reilly provides a good example of this.[17] She invited middle school students to write poems after they had experienced two illustrated books on young refugees and painted collaborative representations of their responses.[18] Javier is the first finished. He brings Mary Ann his poem, which is a single continuous string of words with no punctuation. His home language is Spanish and he has less than three years of English. Mary Ann invites Javier to read his poem to her, and she responds to it with, "Wow! I can see that. What an ending! Read it again." Her feedback establishes that his writing has had an effect on his audience, particularly the way he did his ending. She asks if she can show him something about his poem. He nods his assent, and she turns his attention to the process. "When I listened to you read, I notice that you paused, almost as if there was some punctuation. Yet when I look at the poem, I don't see any. Go ahead and reread your poem out loud. Do you mind if I insert some punctuation as you read?" With his consent, she does so for half of the poem. Then they reread it together. She explains, "Punctuation is nothing more than musical notation for breath. Like directions for a song. I placed that punctuation based on how you read it. I stopped here so that you could continue punctuating the poem. The slashes are possible line breaks." Having established that the writing had an effect on his audience, Mary Ann's feedback continues on the assumption that Javier is a bona fide author who is (a) in control of his work ("Do you mind if I . . ."), and (b) probably interested in information that would help further his intentions (bringing his written version in line with his spoken version). The net effect is to affirm Javier's identity as an author, primarily by taking him seriously as one. The feedback could be construed as corrective, but only within a frame of "getting it right," and that is not the frame Mary Ann opens.

Mary Ann's feedback uses the same model as when a two-year-old, trying to be like his or her parent, attempts modestly successfully to fill a cup from a jug. The feedback would not focus on the spilling but on accomplishing the intention and keeping the identity intact, and might be something like "Wow. That's a big jug. Sometimes it's easier to pour when you . . ." or "You're being very grown up. Can I help you with that?" It is like the comment "How does that feel to complete your first nonfiction book?" The comment establishes the child as a bona fide author by specifying the particular kind of book. At the same time, without force, it sets up the expectation that, given that the child is an author, obviously there will be more such books.

The purpose of feedback is to improve conceptual understanding or increase strategic options while developing stamina, resilience, and motivation—expanding the vision of what is possible and how to get there. Perhaps we should call it *feedforward* rather than feedback. This leads me to say a few words in defense of criticism.

Some Praise for Criticism

I have discussed praise at length, mentioning briefly the problems with criticism. I should make clear, though, that, as with praise, a certain kind of criticism has an important place. Lisa Troyer and Reef Youngreen studied the effects of criticism on creativity.[19] They compared the effects of criticism of the idea with criticism of the person and with no criticism. Criticism of the idea was "I don't like that idea" or "That idea does not seem useful" or "That's not a good idea." Criticism of the source of the idea personalized the criticism by adding "your" and the person's name, for example, "I don't like your idea, Peter." They found that when ideas could be criticized, the group generated more ideas and they were more creative than when either the person could be criticized or even when there was no evaluation at all. The same was true with group members' level of satisfaction. When creativity is high, it turns out to be more satisfying.

I expand this idea in Chapters 5 and 8 in the book, and it will become clear that the idea-focused feedback used by Troyer and Youngreen can be improved upon substantially, beginning with adding the word *because*. But notice how in this research Troyer and Youngreen were concerned about feedback from group members—peer feedback. Anyone who has taught for any length of time or had school-aged children knows that peer feedback can be more powerful than that of the teacher or parent. Indeed, these researchers found that when one group member criticizes the source of the idea, the person, it establishes the rules of the discussion and others begin to do the same. As teachers, using productive forms of feedback is essential, but actually, a change in community talk is equally important. I return to this matter in later chapters.

Formative Assessment

You might have been reading this chapter thinking to yourself, "This is about formative assessment." It is. We use the term *formative* to describe experiences that shape us as we grow up, and a formative assessment is one that shapes learning.[20] The heart of formative assessment is finding the edge of students' learning and helping them to take up possibilities for growth. Assessment isn't formative if it doesn't influence learning in a positive way.

Formative assessment isn't only the teacher's responsibility. In the end, the community members will need to be able to recognize how to take stock of their own and each other's learning and respond to it in ways that provide a productive path forward. However, it is the teacher's responsibility to ensure that the students know how and are disposed to take up their responsibilities for formative assessment. It is the teacher's job to ensure that formative assessment is a property of the learning community and its members. And formative assessment should not merely focus on academic learning, but should include the conditions for community learning. A good example of what this sounds like can be found on page 105. Indeed, as teachers, we need to formatively assess the classroom community's ability to do this.

Fortunately, this isn't as hard as it seems. If we establish a classroom discourse in which people notice and can talk about change with an eye toward possibility, good things will happen. Students tend to take up the language of our interactions with them. But I argue later that if we're going to help students become proficient at formative assessment, we might as well go the whole way. Really, we want to make sure that students know how to teach one another. We need to help them become lifelong teachers as well as lifelong learners.

Any Other Ways to Think About That? Inquiry, Dialogue, Uncertainty, and Difference

The widespread failure to recognize the insights that can be found

in all different perspectives may itself constitute a disability.

—ELLEN LANGER[1]

Consider the following two questions:

    A. The three main reasons for the Civil War were . . .?
    B. From the perspective of the white male living in the twentieth century, the main reasons for the Civil War were . . .?

Question A will not lead to an engaging conversation. Nor will it lead to much learning. In fact, you can almost hear the clatter of minds snapping shut. Although it is a question, it makes clear with the word *the* that there is a correct answer and that our answer will be judged. The question takes as given that there is a single correct answer. Question B is quite different. It is much more likely to lead to an engaging conversation and some learning. Right away it invites comparisons with others' perspectives—women, black men, people in a different century, and so forth. It takes as given that there will be multiple perspectives. It offers uncertainty, and invites mindful engagement.

The difference between the two questions can be thought of as a shift from asking whether something is true to asking when something might be true. This is a pivotal difference for several reasons. First, in the context of previous chapters, you can see that, by insisting that context makes a difference, the second question invites a dynamic theory—in this case about knowledge. Second, it offers uncertainty, and thus enables inquiry. By offering uncertainty and inquiry, it also offers agency with respect to knowledge construction. Third, when students learn that making sense of information requires considering context, they have reason to continue thinking about the information and possible contexts. Fourth, by legitimizing different perspectives, the second question invites dialogue. It recognizes that knowledge is constructed, and that people play an active role in its construction. Question A is monologic. It admits to only one perspective. Turning it into dialogue would require an active rejection of the legitimacy of the question, such as "According to whom?" or "There were many reasons"—a difficult thing to do if the question is asked by a person in a more powerful position, such as the teacher.

Let me unpack these assertions a bit, beginning with dialogue and the dialogic classroom, and explain why these four features of question B are important.

Dialogue

A dialogic classroom is one in which there are lots of open questions and extended exchanges among students. These are not classrooms based on the delivery of facts. They are classrooms in which there are multiple interpretations and perspectives—classrooms in which facts are considered in different contexts and in which people challenge each other's views and conclusions. Even if students agree on a particular fact, they might disagree on its relevance for a particular situation. Remember in Chapter 1, I introduced you to Manny and Sergio discussing *A Picnic in October*? I'll repeat that transcript here:

Manny: No, no, you see, he was rude, but he changed.
Sergio: Rude people don't change. He was making fun of
        everyone; he pretended to throw up . . .
Manny: That's sick!
Sergio: Yeah, but it was because he didn't want to go, he was like
        mad that they made him . . . and embarrassed too, like me
        when my mom makes me go . . .

Manny: Yeah, at first, but look here at the end, see (*flips the pages*)—they're leaving, . . . here it is . . . see, he looks, he looks at the other family—it's like he gets it!

Sergio: Let me see again. (*Grabs book, studies the pictures on the pages Manny showed him, and whisper-reads the words on the pages.*) Oh—you mean like now he gets why the Grandma thinks the statue is a big deal?

Manny: Yeah, now he gets it.

Sergio: So now it's in his heart, too?

Manny: No—well okay, yeah, I guess it could be in his heart, but now he really gets that it's in his grandma's heart.

These two children are engaged in dialogue. They have different perspectives and they negotiate meaning from those perspectives. Their perspectives change in the process. They are focused on meaning making and they are taking responsibility for the (temporary) meaning they have made. Notice that the power relationship between the students is symmetrical rather than the typical asymmetrical expert-novice relationship. Both have something to contribute and to learn. Did I mention that these children are in a school with almost 100 percent subsidized lunch and a high percentage of English language learners?

Looking at conversations like this, it is easy to see why Martin Nystrand and his colleagues found that students in dialogic classrooms "recalled their readings better, understood them in more depth, and responded more fully to aesthetic elements of literature than did students in more typical, monologically organized classes."[2] They also found that dialogic classrooms tended to reduce achievement differences across race, ethnicity, socioeconomic status, and school track. Others have found similar consequences. For example, Kris van den Branden found that such extended discussions are particularly effective at promoting reading comprehension with difficult texts.[3] Indeed, it is exactly those places where there are differences and difficulties that children become engaged in negotiating meaning. And the benefits are not restricted to native speakers. English language learners benefit just as much.[4]

Given these benefits, and the sheer fun of it for teachers and students, you would think that dialogue would be rampant in classrooms across the country. Alas, it is not. Nystrand and his colleagues, in their research on eighth- and ninth-grade English classes, encountered, on average, fifty seconds a day of dialogic interaction in eighth-grade classes and at ninth-grade only fifteen seconds. These average times obscure the fact that in a handful of classes there was a lot of dialogic instruction, but in most, there was none.[5] I will explore the reasons for this presently, but for now, let's think about what a dialogic classroom sounds like with the teacher involved. Maria Nichols[6] reports that the following dialogue took place in Cheryl McMann's fifth-grade class when they were discussing the book *Stealing Home: Jackie Robinson: Against the Odds*.[7] The book section describes Jackie Robinson, the first African American professional baseball player, joining the Brooklyn Dodgers. The manager comments that he is "looking for a ballplayer with guts enough not to fight back" in the face of expected racial slurs and taunts. The students take up the discussion as follows:

Joshua: He said he'll need guts—that's saying courage—because white people won't like that he's getting to play.

Cheryl: So why do you think Jackie agreed? What does this tell us about him?

Joshua: He said yes so he can play.

Jonathan: No, no, I think . . .

Cheryl: Ah, Jonathan, it sounds like you have a different idea?

Jonathan: (*Shakes head yes.*)

Cheryl: Will you hold on to it until we dig into Joshua's idea? Let's hear his evidence before we move on to a new idea. Joshua, what makes you think that's the reason?

Joshua: Because he was the star in college—but he couldn't be on a team because of racism.

Cheryl: What do the rest of you think?

Kayla: It said that was how the world was back then. So he had to say yes, because he could get a chance (*to play*). He couldn't get a chance before. They didn't care he was the star because he was black.

Jonathan: But Kayla, he . . . well, he . . . yeah, he probably did want to play, but it's like Martin Luther King Jr. He always said don't fight. And the book said . . .

Theresea: Oh! It's like *The Other Side* (*referring to the book by Jacqueline Woodson, which the students had read, thought, and talked about together*)! It said about the wall—on the other page (*referring to the "Then and Now" section*). It's like the fence. He (*Jackie Robinson*) knows it shouldn't be.

Marta: Oh, yeah. I didn't think about that!

Cheryl: So you're constructing a new theory for why Jackie agreed not to fight back. What does everyone think about this idea (*looking questioningly around the circle*)?

Ben: No, I don't get it—what Theresea said.

Cheryl: When you don't understand what someone said, remember, it's your job to ask them to explain.

Ben: (*looking at Theresea*) I don't get what you mean.

This is a small section of the conversation, and already there's some dialogue. Let's think about the strategies Cheryl uses to build the conversation. Four students respond to each other without Cheryl breaking the chain of engagement. In most classrooms, the students would all speak through her, but she keeps herself out of this controlling position. How?

First, she asks open questions: "So why do you think. . ." By inquiring into students' "thinking," she invites them to make their draft thinking process available rather than provide facts. At the same time this helps develop the children's "mind reading"—their ability to imagine themselves into other's heads—which we will take up in Chapter 6. Second, she gives enough wait time so that others will respond. Third, she does not judge the children's ideas. There is no "yes," "good," and so on. Instead, she invites others to respond: "What do the rest of you think?" "What does everyone think about this idea?" Fourth, notice that she doesn't specify who will be allowed to respond, which again keeps her out of the controlling position. Fifth, in each response she shows that she takes their ideas seriously and is listening to them. We see this partly in her use of "So . . ." as she bases her response on what they have said. We also see it when she asks Jonathan respectfully to hold on to his idea temporarily ("until") so they can seriously pursue another student's idea. She gives a reason—because they can only "dig into," or take one idea seriously, at a time. In other words, Cheryl positions the students as knowledgeable, thinking individuals who can manage their conversational turn taking—and they do the same to each other. Sixth, when she wants to get an idea considered, she uses tentativeness markers ("I'm wondering if . . ." "Could Jackie . . .") to show a degree of uncertainty and reduce her positional authority.

Each of these decisions keeps her out of the controlling position, leaving a more symmetrical power arrangement. Students do not feel motivated to compete for her attention. Nonetheless, after one of her comments, Ben turns to her to say that he doesn't understand what Theresea said. She promptly reminds him that this issue is between him and Theresea. So he turns and looks at Theresea and asks for clarification. As he does this in the future, he will show others that he is taking them seriously, respecting them as contributing thinkers. At the same time, the habit of making sure that he understands others will expand his mind reading—and his social network. Because things that we don't yet understand offer points of disjuncture, they are often places where learning can take place. In this overall conversation, Cheryl is offering students a narrative of who they are and what they are doing. They are "digging into" ideas—an activity that requires all of them—and they are all respected, contributing thinkers. After a few more student comments, Cheryl poses their shared intellectual problem by summarizing the current possibilities in their collective mind:

> *So, we have two different points of view. We're thinking Jackie may have agreed not to fight back so he could play baseball on a professional team, or maybe he said yes to prove racism is wrong. What do the rest of you think?*

She then asks them to turn and talk, and, in the process, sets them up to take each other seriously and clarify their thinking further. Notice, again, that doing so will require them to imagine Jackie's thinking—to mind read. Appendix A is an expanded turn-by-turn analysis of this set of interactions. Strategies for arranging such conversations are summarized in Figure 5.1.

I hope you can see from the conversation in Cheryl's class that books are not merely to entertain or to teach kids to figure out words or even to learn things from. They are tools for growing minds. Liz Yanoff began her first-grade research referring to "read aloud" or "story

---

Figure 5.1 Tools for Reducing Asymmetrical Power Relationships

- Ask open questions—questions that could have multiple answers.
- Use uncertainty markers: *maybe, perhaps, I wonder.*
- Offer ample wait time.
- Do not judge ideas: ~~yes, good, well . . . , right.~~
- Arrange for class members to manage turn taking without you.
- Do not repeat children's good ideas so the class can hear them.
- Ask children to report to the class what their partner had to say rather than what they themselves had to say.
- Remind children to speak directly to each other rather than through you.
- Position the students in a circle so they can speak and listen to each other and see each other's reactions.
- Position yourself physically as much as possible at the same level, and either in the circle with the students or outside it.

time" but quickly realized that it would be more accurate to say that it was time for "reading together" or, more accurately, "thinking together with books."[8] The fact that the teacher is reading aloud is not the central feature of the activity.

Although I have explained how Cheryl built dialogue in her classroom, most of us find these strategies hard to use because we were raised in a monologic world. We often find it hard not to respond to students' comments with "good," "right," or "weelll . . ." Similarly, when students ask us a question or present a problem to us, we can't seem to help answering it or solving it rather than supporting them in answering or solving it themselves. Some teachers stop their judgment using a nonjudgmental "Hmmmm," as they look expectantly around at the children's faces and wait for someone to pick up the idea that is on the table. Judith Lindfors observes that dialogue is a bit like a game in which keeping the ball in play is the goal rather than winning.[9] Indeed, by focusing on the process more than the outcome, these students are led into a dynamic frame—this time with respect to knowledge rather than characteristics of people. They understand that knowledge is constructed, that it is influenced by one's perspective and by different contexts, and that we should expect and value different perspectives because they help us to expand our understanding. As Robert Altman is quoted as saying, "If you and I agreed about everything, then one of us is unnecessary."[10] Similarly, just as there is a fixed frame with respect to characteristics of people, there is a fixed frame regarding the characteristics of knowledge. I present these contrasting frames in Figure 5.2.

Students in dialogic classrooms come to value their conversations because they are engaging and because they learn from them. Indeed, when Terri Thorkildson asked children in such classrooms how they viewed conversations, the children thought that the conversations were essential, particularly because of their learning. When she asked them about tests, the children felt that tests simply interfered with the conversations. When she asked the same question in a direct-instruction classroom, the children thought the reverse. Without the tests, they could see no reason to learn, and the conversations would just take up time when they could be being taught. Besides, one child observed, in a discussion, you might give others the answers.[11]

Although children in dialogic classrooms may have productive conversations, they are not necessarily aware of some of the important aspects of the conversations. For example, unless Manny and Sergio's teacher helped them notice that they had just disagreed (see pages 52–53) and how their disagreement helped them to learn, I doubt they

Figure 5.2 Dynamic vs. Fixed View of Knowledge

Individual Beliefs and Behaviors

Dynamic Knowledge Frame	Fixed Knowledge Frame
Believe knowledge is growing, changing, and likely to be affected by context and perspective.	Believe knowledge is a collection of facts that are not affected by context. Have a strong desire for stability and certainty—knowledge that everyone agrees with.
Even after having made up their mind about an issue, they are prepared to consider new information or different perspectives and change.	Judge ideas quickly based on the most accessible quality and cling to that judgment regardless of new information and particularly in the face of minority perspectives.
When considering conflict situations can understand the perspective of both sides.	View conflict situations as black/white, right/wrong.
View open questions that are amenable to a range of answers and perspectives as most interesting. Find uncertainty and novelty interesting.	Avoid uncertainty and unpredictable situations, including open questions that can be answered in different ways.
Enjoy interacting with people whose opinions are very different from their own.	Prefer to socialize with familiar friends and people who think similarly.
When thinking about a problem, consider as many different opinions as possible.	Decide on a solution, seek confirming evidence, and avoid conflicting opinions.
Are interested in multiple perspectives.	Become annoyed when one person disagrees with what others in the group think.
Feel that changing plans can be exciting.	Hate changing plans.
Think that controversial topics and books are good places for interesting conversations.	Avoid controversial topics or books.

would even recall having disagreed, let alone come to value it as a source of learning. They would just recall the conversation as a satisfying experience of thinking together about a book. So, we offer a narrative that helps children recall the value of difference and how they can make such conversations possible. Cheryl might say, for example, "Look what happened when we had more than one way to think about Jackie Robinson. We had an interesting discussion, thinking about the story—well, about history—more deeply. I notice that often happens when we disagree and listen carefully to each other."

Through conversations like this, the students come to understand this kind of conversation as collaborative inquiry. Though each person sometimes speaks with authority, there is more tentativeness and a developing awareness that making sense often requires more than one person. They have a sense that they are stretching into their zone of proximal development. It is as if they are stretching to that next rock in the stream and become aware they need to reach out to others for a balancing hand. The language they use to reach out includes tentativeness markers like *maybe, or something, perhaps, could be,* and sort of. These markers point to uncertainty. The problem with "the three reasons for the Civil War" is that there is no uncertainty. The knowledge is already made. It is fixed. There is nothing to be done, no sense to be made, no possibility of agency.

Uncertainty, Inquiry, and Meaning Making

It is the perception of uncertainty that enables dialogue. Dialogue, in turn, sustains uncertainty. If there is certainty, or only one view, there is nothing to discuss and nothing to learn. Uncertainty is the foundation of inquiry and research. Unfortunately, most conversations about schooling work from the assumption that a curriculum is a bunch of certain facts to be efficiently delivered to the students, and that a teacher's problem is to deliver the true facts so that they stick, are well organized, and can be assessed. Because they are facts, there should be no disagreement. The unfortunate problem with facts is that they are generally inert and thus uninteresting. Oh, it's true that we find unusual facts interesting, like the fact that it's impossible to sneeze with your eyes open,[12] or that men can read smaller print than women, but women can hear better.[13] But the reason these facts are interesting is that they raise so many new questions.

Most of us were schooled in monologic classrooms and, in the process, we learned to value facts and certainty. We acquired a fixed view of knowledge. We say "America is a democracy." When we deliver information to students with *is* we invoke a fixed frame. We say, in effect, that teaching is about giving these facts about the world, and learning is about receiving them. When students take up information like that, they have no reason to check it. An authority delivered it as a fact. They also have no reason to think about it any further—unless there's a test, and even then they don't actually think about it; they only check that they recall it correctly. Notice the way the statement positions us, too. Our students are positioned as the baby birds with their mouths open for knowledge and the teacher does all the work bringing the knowledge to drop into their waiting beaks—at least when they are hungry for the knowledge. The student is not in a position to contribute and not set up to go looking for knowledge. In this frame, there is no agency in knowledge production. Introducing uncertainty is not so difficult. We could say, "Some people view America as a democracy; others view it as a republic. What's your view?" or "In what ways might America be considered a democracy?"

In other words, just as we learn fixed and dynamic theories about people, we learn fixed and dynamic theories about knowledge. Those of us who grew up in monologic classrooms were socialized into fixed theories. We learned to value and seek stability and closure. We learned to feel uncomfortable with uncertainty, so we tend to make what Ellen Langer calls "premature cognitive commitments," that is, a "rigid belief that results from the mindless acceptance of information as true without consideration of alternative versions of that information." Premature cognitive commitment locks people into a particular version of information or reality when other versions might work better in different situations. "People do not reconsider," Langer observes, "what they mindlessly accepted as true."[14]

Premature cognitive commitments occur more often when the information is presented as fact (*is*) rather than as possibility (*could be*), when the information is presented as irrelevant rather than as relevant, and when the context suggests that it is not necessary to reexamine the information, such as when an authority presents it. Just changing our language from *is* to *could be* changes a great deal. Ellen Langer describes a study in which two groups of college students were presented with some items: a polygraph pen, a hair dryer attachment, and a piece of a dog's chew toy. One group was introduced to each item with "This is a . . . ," whereas the other group was introduced to them with "This could be a . . ." Later, students in both groups were put in a position in which it might be possible to use the objects to solve problems, but only by using them flexibly, in ways inconsistent with their label. Only members of the "could be" group were able to use the items flexibly, such as using a dog's chew toy as an eraser.[15] Just saying "could be" instead of "is" liberates potential tools from their categorical cages. Just introducing an element of uncertainty makes tools, and knowledge, more flexible. Uncertainty, then, can have an advantage in developing flexibility and creative use of knowledge.

Judith Lindfors observes that dialogue is "a continual balancing act in which participants move between being in balance and off balance. Inquiry utterances are the quintessential off-balance moves in a dialogue. They disrupt; they destabilize." As with change (which has its own uncertainties), to be comfortably uncertain about some things we need to have a degree of certainty in others. In particular, as I noted earlier, security about self-worth seems to be a necessary anchor.[16] We need to be certain that we are okay whether or not we are successful, are confused, or make mistakes. This means showing our students our own comfort with uncertainty; insisting that students focus their uncertainty, share it, and capitalize on it; explaining why it is useful to do so; and publicly and positively noticing it when students demonstrate their comfort with uncertainty.

These ways in which we approach uncertainty in the classroom are important. In concluding one (of several) discussions of *Martin's Big Words* with her first graders, Pegeen Jensen capitalized on one particular page—the page where Doreen Rappaport's text says "He died." Brian Collier's illustration is especially evocative, and prompted a range of interpretations. Rather than resolving the discussion, Pegeen said, "Possibly. I'm going to leave this page open. Right here. Whew. If you have any other thoughts about this really interesting picture, would you put it on a Post-it and leave it here for us? Because I think we're still confused a little bit about this picture or we might want to share more about it." Throughout the day children returned to wonder and comment.[17] Pegeen showed her valuing of uncertainty and wonder, and the continued thinking that it provoked. In this same classroom, Liz Yanoff and two students were thinking through *Grandfather Twilight*,[18] also an evocative book, and wondering about the grandfather. Liz commented, "Yea . . . This is one of those books that you have . . . people have a lot of questions about this book. Are all of our questions answered by the words?" Bryon, one of the students, asserted that they are not. He then observed, quite comfortably, "Sometimes they don't have the answers."

Jeralyn Johnson insists that her fourth graders recognize and share their own uncertainties. When they were discussing a math problem in pairs and threes, she noted, "If you're confused, there should be a conversation about your confusion, right? Like, 'I understand it's the hundreds below, not the thousands. I don't understand this part. Help me out.' I should hear a conversation about your confusion." When a student focused his confusion during class discussion, she observed, "Do you see how he didn't just tell me he didn't know the answer? He did tell me what he did know. Why is that important?"

Among the answers offered, a student observed, "He just didn't give up."

Jeralyn listened to their comments without judging, and then added, "And now I can help him. Because I know what he does understand, so I can help him with the part he doesn't understand. If you just say, 'I don't get it,' then how do I help you? How do you help yourself? Okay, so Jose, you said you do know seven times three? Then what are your thoughts about that other part?" This is how some children more than others acquire a greater comfort with uncertainty, and the consequences are worth contemplating.

Need for Closure

For some people more than others, uncertainty is unsettling. They would like to have simple facts, consensus, and uniformity of ideas. Researchers refer to this as a need for closure. Individuals with a high need for closure tend to judge ideas quickly based on the most accessible quality and cling to that judgment regardless of subsequent information. This is often referred to as "seizing and freezing." If these individuals enter a conversation with an opinion on the topic, they freeze to it and refuse to consider other views. If they don't have an opinion, they are easily persuaded to their partner's opinion, seizing it and freezing to it.[19] They have a strong desire for knowledge that everyone agrees on, and that offers stability and certainty.[20] Because of this desire, their behavior in group discussions is problematic. Their relationships with others are affected. They reject those who threaten stable consensus by disagreeing. They become annoyed and even hostile towards toward them. They evaluate conformists in the group more positively than they do those who express or defend conflicting ideas. In other words, they behave in ways that systematically undermine dialogue—and undermine a productive learning community.

I am beginning to sound as though need for closure is a fixed characteristic of people. It isn't. Just as children come to us with different dispositions toward fixed-performance or dynamic-learning frames, they come to us socialized into different degrees of need for closure. However, as with the fixed and dynamic frames, need for closure is also socialized and situational. We can change children's comfort with uncertainty by changing the conversational structures that fill their lives, or by changing the situation. Stresses such as time pressure or noise reliably increase need for closure. I'm sure other stresses, like high-stakes testing, work just as well to increase need for closure. On the other hand, dialogic instruction is an excellent antidote, as one eighth-grade student commented to Heather Lattimer after a semester in a dialogic class:[21]

> *Before I wouldn't ever be interested in discussing serious things really. I wasn't the person to sit down and just have a discussion about things, like, that's what I wanted, that's my mind-set, I'm not going to change. Now it's like, you have to listen to both sides. When someone says something I don't agree with, I want to talk about it. That's what the class—that's what I learned throughout the class.*

Perhaps you think I am overstating the case for increasing children's comfort with uncertainty. But I have not yet described the consequences of groups of people who all have a high need for closure or whose group is under pressures that increase everyone's need for closure (studies have been done with both situations with equivalent results). To begin with, when need for closure is increased in a group, the power symmetry of the group changes. Some group members hog the floor, having more to say and more said to them, and they have a greater influence on the views of other group members.[22] Group interactions shift toward increased authoritarianism.[23] Individuals pressure other group members to conform.[24] They develop more autocratic views, view autocratic leaders more favorably, and shift toward autocratic group leadership.[25] In other words, group processes, and group members, become less egalitarian, less democratic. I don't want to alarm you, but high need to reduce uncertainty and ambiguity has been linked to the emergence of authoritarian regimes and fundamentalist belief systems.[26] But there's more.

With increased need for closure, people also begin to develop a bias toward their in-group and against others who are different,[27] particularly when they view group members as similar to themselves.[28] When they don't view group members as similar because they disagree, they exclude these group members in order to maintain their sense of group similarity and shared reality.[29] This "group-centrism" shows up in laboratory studies and in real-world settings, such as ethnic groups and immigrant assimilation.[30] Doesn't this remind you of some of the consequences of the fixed-performance frame, such as the increased tendency to stereotype? Doesn't the rejection of difference remind you of the rejection of challenge that occurs in the fixed-performance frame? In every way, need for closure disrupts dialogic communities by reducing the expression of diverse perspectives and disrupting the social support system. It reduces creativity and limits opportunities for learning and adapting. These consequences are presented in Figure 5.3.

In my view, we have ample grounds for the kind of dialogic teaching interactions I have described, which value uncertainty and

Figure 5.3 Dynamic vs. Fixed View of Knowledge

Group Behaviors

Dynamic Knowledge Frame	Fixed Knowledge Frame
Are comfortable with difference, expect it, and value the engagement it provides.	Reject and show animosity toward those who threaten stable group consensus by disagreeing.
Demonstrate efforts to understand, engage, and persuade.	Pressure group members to conform.
Find difference engaging, and when difference is engaged in discussion, it results in an enhanced view of other group members.	Judge conformists in their group more positively than dissenters.
Resist autocratic interaction patterns; favor democratic patterns and perspective.	Favor and adopt autocratic interaction patterns and perspective.
Attend to and engage difference in the group; perceive more in-group difference and thus avoid simple contrast with those outside the group.	Show a bias toward (and overestimation of) in-group, and against others who are different, particularly when they view group members as similar to themselves.

reduce the rush to closure. Socializing children into a greater tolerance for uncertainty seems sensible for their own development and for the benefit of society, and because, frankly, it will make classroom management easier and children happier. A greater tolerance for uncertainty brings with it a greater tolerance for others. The same research suggests that increasing the stress on schools, such as through high-stakes testing, is ill advised. Indeed, researchers have shown that stress increases what Irving Janis called "groupthink." There are three entirely consistent characteristics of groupthink: closed-mindedness, pressure toward uniformity, and overestimation of the in-group.[31] We have to begin to recognize that increasing pressure on teachers will not lead to productive learning. In fact, the root of *school* is in the Greek word *schola*, meaning "leisure." Time for extended dialogic conversation is critical.

Disagreement, Disjuncture, and Diversity

For intellectual development, the most powerful lever comes when children disagree and take each other seriously. We saw examples of this with Manny and Sergio and in the Jackie Robinson conversation at the beginning of the chapter. I offer another example. After an extended discussion about why two ducklings born in the classroom were pecking a third, one fourth grader made the following extended statement:

> *I disagree with Shirley because [provides evidence] and I agree with Jack and Gordon because [makes an observation], and [another observation] . . . So [offers a hypothesis] because [another observation] But [another observation].*[32]

The complexity of this comment is astonishing. It required the student to have attended to many other perspectives as well as to evidence, to hypothesize about the evidence, and to synthesize a conclusion. Notice the language—*because, so, but, and*—all logical connectors that will show up in persuasive writing (she was attempting here to persuade), but also in math, science, and social studies.

Direct instruction will not produce this thinking. It requires a conversation in which equals publicly disagree. Vygotsky argued that cognitive growth is "more likely when one is required to explain, elaborate, or defend one's position to others as well as to oneself; striving for an explanation often makes a learner integrate and elaborate knowledge in new ways."[33] Piaget also weighed in on this. He taught us the power of disjuncture in forcing children to revise their theories. He also felt that disjuncture was most useful when confronted in a symmetrical power space.[34] If a teacher delivered conflicting information, Piaget felt that children were more likely to simply accept the information delivered by an authority without having to actually wrestle with the conflict. Symmetrical power situations are also important for normalizing in children a sense of self-respect and developing a resistance to being "put down."

Remember that a fixed-performance frame in the classroom will undermine productive disagreement, because disagreement signals that one party must be wrong and being wrong is an indicator of one's (permanent) lack of ability. People deal with this by putting down the other person. A fixed-knowledge frame will produce similar results. This is why we normalize the expectation and valuing of difference. We ask, "Are there any other ways to think about this?" and "Hmm. What do you others think?" It is why we use books like Anthony Browne's *Voices in the Park*,[35] which make multiple perspectives explicit. It is why we use multiple text sets that offer a range of perspectives rather than single texts (for good examples, see Maria Nichols and Kathy Short).[36] It is why we help children expect to explain and defend their positions to others—in all curriculum areas. For example, when Andie Smith joined a pair of her students working together to solve a math problem involving the number line and rounding, she said, "You're a fabulous team. . . . How did you know that forty-eight came between forty-five and fifty? . . . Why did you decide to round up? . . . Do you agree with her? . . . Why? . . . You knew it was . . . but how did you know it was . . .?"

When people expect to disagree and to explain their position, have a reasonable tolerance for and expectation of uncertainty, understand the value of listening to others, particularly those who think differently, and work to produce symmetrical power relationships, they are well prepared for a strong democracy. If we want these characteristics in our school graduates, dialogic instruction is the way to go. Oh, yes, and they'll do better on tests and the gaps among subgroups of the population will tend to close.[37] And they'll become more critically literate. On the other hand, if we want children to leave school with closed minds, have an inclination to surround themselves with people who think the same as they do, have a tendency to stereotype and exclude those who are different, be unable to voice or tolerate dissent, and lean toward an autocratic and authoritarian view of the world, well, we also know what to do.

Social Imagination

*If you can learn a simple trick, Scout, you'll get along a lot better
with all kinds of folks. You never really understand a person until
you consider things from his point of view . . . until you climb inside
of his skin and walk around in it.*

　　　　　　　　　—ATTICUS FINCH IN *To Kill a Mockingbird*[1]

In the beginning of this book I promised to show you how the language
we choose in our teaching changes the worlds children inhabit now and
the worlds they will build in the future. Although their cognitive development is, of course, critical, we have to take seriously the fact that
human beings are fundamentally social animals.[2] Our life form is such
that children deprived of social interaction not only won't thrive but
also will literally wither and die.[3] Learning is fundamentally social. At
the basic level, if a student is unable to successfully recruit assistance or
jointly participate in activities, learning will suffer. Social development
is the foundation for intellectual, emotional, and physical health, even
in adulthood. Although curriculum developers often act as if these
dimensions of development are separate, only by pretending that children are not human beings can we avoid attending to this inseparable
wholeness. In Chapter 2, for example, I showed that when children
adopt a fixed frame, it affects their intellectual lives (e.g., they avoid
challenging tasks), their emotional lives (e.g., they more easily become
depressed), their social lives (e.g., they blame others for failure and put
partners down when they have different perspectives), and their moral
lives (e.g., they tend to stereotype, to justify cheating, and to be punitive).

In Chapter 5, I showed how a fixed-knowledge frame has a similar range of effects. In this chapter, we will explore another key link among social, emotional, moral, and intellectual development. First, an example.

Maria Nichols reports the following conversations in Jesse Harrison's third-grade class.[4] Jesse is reading with her students the book *The Summer My Father Was Ten* by Pat Brisson. The book is a child's retelling of a father's reflection on a mistake he made as a ten-year-old. While playing baseball with his friends, the ball lands by his elderly neighbor's garden. In a moment of mischief, he throws back a tomato instead of the ball, an act that escalates and results in the destruction of the garden. The following year his neighbor doesn't plant a garden.

> **Jesse:** (*teacher—reading from text*) *but still, Mr. Bellavista made no move to plant.*
>
> **Darcie:** Probably Mr. Bellavista hasn't started to plant because he's scared to.
>
> **Jasmine:** Oh! I was thinking the same thing! Mr. Bellavista thinks that if he plants again, the boys will go in and play and ruin the garden again.
>
> **Many voices:** Oh! Oh yeah! (*Hands shooting up*) . . . That's what I think too . . . yeah, you had my same idea . . . it has to be because in the picture . . .
>
> **Jesse:** OK, OK, turn and talk—what makes you think this is what Mr. Bellavista is thinking?

Later, in the book, when the boy wants to apologize, Jesse pauses again:

> **Jesse:** (*reading from text*) . . . *but he just couldn't make the words come out.*
>
> **Benjamin:** He looks at the empty lot and he can't forget because he knows it shouldn't be empty.
>
> **Damon:** Yeah, he can't get it out of his mind. It's so sad.
>
> **Jesse:** Oh, why so sad?
>
> **Damon:** It's because a garden should be there, but they wrecked it, and the other sad part is when you want to say "sorry" but you can't, it's, like, like it said, his body won't go.
>
> **Andre:** It's like your brain knows, it's trying, but your body can't.
>
> **Keysha:** In his heart I think he feels like he needs to say sorry. His heart is pumping really hard, and he feels very nervous.

Diana: Yeah, I felt that before. Just like it said, the words, they won't—it's too hard to say them.

Keysha: Sometimes I can't say sorry because I don't know why I did something, so I'm nervous and scared. But I feel bad.

Shante: Yeah, that's how he is—the father—he knows how they shouldn't have wrecked the garden, and doesn't know why they all did it. He knows what he has to do, but it's hard. He feels bad. But he has courage to follow his heart.

Such conversations can be justified on academic grounds because they develop children's comprehension, particularly of complex narratives.[5] They also build a depth of engagement that will lead to more reading, perhaps repeated reading, and to more conversations—all excellent reasons for choosing books that provoke such conversations, and for teaching children how to build these conversations (which we'll get to in Chapter 8). However, to understand the full importance of such conversations, we have to think about what the conversation requires of students. Darcie starts by imagining that Mr. Bellavista's motive for not planting is that he is scared, and she makes it available for others' thinking. Others follow her lead and take up residence in the minds of the characters. The significance of this is easily missed.

The problem with apprenticing children into humanity—the intellectual and social life of society—is that much of the action we want them to understand takes place inside people's heads. We have to help them learn to imagine what goes on inside heads, and not just the cognitive strategies being used to solve problems, but the complex social-emotional logic that lies behind their behavior. Actually, human beings are born with a propensity to do this. For example, if a child between about three months and eighteen months is playing with a toy and you cover the toy with your hand, the first thing the child will do is look at your face to try to figure out what you think you're doing. The child assumes you are acting intentionally, that something is going on in your head, so she tries to read your mind from the available cues. But not all children develop this ability as quickly or as well as others. A child with autism of about the same mental age is more likely to simply view your hand as an obstacle and try to get at the toy without looking at your face for reasons.[6] In other words, although this social imagination is a human propensity, there is individual variability in the starting point and in the rate of development. Development depends on social interactions like those Jesse is sponsoring in her classroom. But there is more to this than meets the eye, so let me explain a little more.

Mind Reading

There are two main dimensions of social imagination. The first is what the baby is trying to do when you cover the toy—read in your face what's going on behind your face. Though research on this goes under a number of names, I'll call it mind reading. This social-perceptual ability begins development in the first year of life, when children start to view others' actions as intentional. Researchers assess the development of this ability in older children and adults by showing them photographs of the eye region of faces and having them figure out the person's mental state.[7] If your interest is in purely academic learning (whatever that might be), then this won't be of much interest to you except that students who are not very good at reading faces will cause more disruptions in class because of their social behavior.[8] And, to the extent that all learning is social, their inability to read in faces (and other body signals) what's going on in others' minds will impact their academic learning.

Fortunately, we can help children develop mind reading without breaking our teaching stride. For example, Jeralyn Johnson, posing a math problem to her fourth graders, says, "Okay, here's your challenge—Antonio is looking at me with a 'bring it on' look."

Later, when she introduces a book she's about to read with her students—*The Wretched Stone* by Chris Van Allsburg—she says, "When I picked up this book I made this face. What was I thinking?"

The students make a concerted effort to use what they know about their teacher and her facial expression to figure out what's going on in her mind. One responds, "Sneaky."

Another offers, "You're going to push us."

On the face of it, it seems like perhaps a little salesmanship to draw in her students. No doubt it has that effect. However, it also has the effect of turning their attention to important social cues and building the connection between those cues and social-emotional activity. When Jeralyn subsequently checks the students' understanding of the word *fascinated* in the book, she reads, "The crew is fascinated by the rock," and asks, "What does that mean?" Various definitions are offered, and she says, "Show me 'fascinated.'" They all focus on the experience of being fascinated and compose their faces to show it.

Susie Althof uses a similar practice when she says to her kindergartners, "Make eye contact and show him that you are listening." She says this when one of them is acting as the teacher for the others. She also says it when they are talking with each other in turn-and-talks, and when she is helping them solve social problems by explaining their problem to each other. The skill (and disposition) these teachers are building will serve the children well in their relationships in the classroom and beyond. It will build the children's reciprocity and simplify classroom management. When they grow up it will serve them well in their personal and professional relationships.[9] It might or might not have a direct impact on their reading or writing, but it forms the basis for a second dimension that will: social reasoning.

Social Reasoning

The second dimension of social imagination is one that you will more easily recognize as having an academic component. This is the ability to imagine and reason about other's actions, intentions, feelings, and beliefs from multiple perspectives.[10] This dimension is slower to develop than its foundation mind reading, partly because it is dependent on the child's expanding ability with language.

At around age four, children begin to realize that a verb can take an entire sentence as a complement: "He thought [the candy was in the jar]." They also begin to grasp that the embedded sentence can be true from one person's point of view, but not from another's. This ability to represent more than one world at once opens important possibilities. The conversation in Jesse's class offers an example. Benjamin observes, "He looks at the empty lot and he can't forget because he knows it shouldn't be empty." To say this, he imagines another mind, and from the perspective of that mind imagines two different worlds, the one that is and the one that isn't. Reducing this to "inference-making" as part of comprehension underestimates its significance, as we shall see. But first, let me say a bit about how to expand social imagination.

You can't teach this dimension of development by telling. Explicit teaching about it in stories, providing metacognitive language about it, does not improve its development. Children have to actively construct their own linguistic representations of people's thinking, and the way we talk or arrange for talk can invite and facilitate these constructions. Conversations in which children disagree or are asked for clarification of what they say are helpful. Reflective conversations about such interactions expand their effectiveness by recognizing the fact of multiple perspectives, and by requiring children to construct sentences that have embedded potentially false worlds, such as when a child observes that a peer (or a book character) "must have thought nobody was watching."[11]

Books are a great vehicle for inviting such sentence constructions.[12] Books like *No, David!* by David Shannon are excellent for inviting children to explore conflicting worlds and false beliefs, such as when an illustration shows David pulling the cat's tail and saying, "But she likes it!" Jeralyn provides another kind of opportunity in math when different groups of students have arrived at different answers to a problem. She asks the class to figure out how someone would arrive at each incorrect answer. To do this, they work through the problem and locate the misconception that led to the answer. Not only does this build social imagination, but it turns students' attention to the process, rehearses cross-checking, and establishes that the final incorrect answer can result from a process that is almost all correct but contains a single misconception ("must have thought that") or slip-up. All are outcomes we know to be positive.

Taking Social Imagination Seriously

Unfortunately, because most normal adults make many basic social inferences automatically, we take social imagination for granted. In spite of widespread interest in books that promise how to tell "whether she's interested" or "whether he's 'into you,'" we tend not to think of social imagination as part of schooling. But social imagination is the foundation of civil society. It is what makes relationships work (or not) and it is the foundation of legal and political practices. It should not be taken for granted. There are considerable individual differences in our ability to make sense of social cues and to think through their implications, and those differences have consequences for children's lives now and for the futures they construct.

Academic Learning

In blunt academic terms, social imagination directly affects the child's ability to comprehend complex narratives. Furthermore, at least in five- to seven-year-olds, social imagination predicts the ability to understand idiomatic expressions like "You're pulling my leg" or "He's up against the wall."[13] With expressions like these, children have to understand that a speaker or writer can intend something other than the literal meaning. Understanding irony depends partly on language development, but it also depends on social imagination, for similar reasons. For example, irony can require a reader to recognize an incongruity between what characters in a book are saying and the situation they are in, and to know that the characters don't recognize the incongruity. For those of you familiar with children's books, think about children coming to understand the Amelia Bedelia series. This requires simultaneously thinking through another's perspective and one's own.[14] Critical literacy requires imagining others' intentions, adopting multiple perspectives, and imagining social arrangements that don't yet exist. Writers or speakers attempting to persuade an audience are more likely to be effective if they can imagine the feelings, reactions, and motives of their audience. The benefits of social imagination for writing fiction are too obvious to mention. But there are many more benefits of a developed social imagination that will certainly affect school life and beyond.

Social Relationships

The more developed a person's social imagination, the higher their level of social cooperation, the larger their social network, and the more positively they are viewed by their peers.[15] Children with well-developed social imaginations have, according to their teachers, more positive social skills than those who do not.[16] In fact, well-developed social imagination is closely related to a whole constellation of positive attributes. In particular, it is related to one of the "big five" measures of "personality": agreeableness. This is a measure of friendliness, warmth, altruism, and attentiveness to others' needs. Friendliness, in turn, is closely related to the degree of social support a person enjoys and the extent to which they experience harmonious relationships.

The more children recognize that others routinely have different perspectives—not just physical perspectives, but emotional, motivational, and cultural perspectives—the more developed they become, socially and morally as well as intellectually. One eighth grader's observation suggests how this might work. She found herself with a long-time acquaintance in a dialogic class for the first time and found that they often disagreed with one another. She observed in an interview with Heather Lattimer, "I think it has made us closer because we like to argue with each other and we know both of each other's sides and stuff like that. So I think it makes us closer."[17] This experience was not unique, and Heather Lattimer notes that, at the end of the semester, many of the students reported that their best friends were now people in the class.

Moral Reasoning

Children's development of social imagination also is related to their development of moral reasoning—their ability to make moral distinctions on the basis of inferred motive—which, in turn, is linked to their prosocial behavior. As students develop a deeper understanding of social-emotional life and personal change, they become less likely to judge people, including themselves, or to develop problems of depression.[18] We will explore the links to moral reasoning in more detail in Chapter 7.

Self-Regulation

Children's self-regulation also develops with expanded social imagination.[19] The conversation in Jesse's class about *The Summer My Father Was Ten* provides a hint as to how social imagination and self-regulation are linked. Keysha demonstrated her social imagination by observing, "In his heart I think he feels like he needs to say sorry. His heart is pumping really hard, and he feels very nervous." She follows this with "Sometimes I can't say sorry because I don't know why I did something, so I'm nervous and scared. But I feel bad." She has imagined another's feelings, motives, and actions, and is using that reflexively to understand and manage her own feelings, motives, and actions. Young children's self-regulation is stronger when their parents engage them in talk about what people are thinking and feeling and when they encourage them to take control of their decision making.[20] Expanding social imagination, along with skill at thinking together, ensure that collaborative activities become increasingly low maintenance. When interpersonal coordination goes well, students' subsequent self-regulation improves. On the other hand, when collaborative activities are high maintenance, students' subsequent self-regulation is impaired.[21]

It is worth remembering that undeveloped self-regulation underlies ADHD.[22] I mention this because researchers from the National Centers for Disease Control and Prevention report that over the twelve years preceding 2008, the incidence of ADHD increased by 33.0 percent and the incidence of autism increased by 289.5 percent.[23]

Behavior Problems

If these positive reasons are not enough to persuade you that developing children's social imagination is important, perhaps the consequences of not developing it will be persuasive. For example, children

who behave badly generally do not have well-developed social imaginations.[24] Indeed, a poorly developed social imagination is related to misbehavior at home and at school, and to angry responses in personal
interactions.[25] Underdeveloped social imagination and moral reasoning
are also linked to aggressive behavior in children.[26] Children who regularly behave aggressively tend to have less well developed, and often dis-
torted, social imaginations. They persistently imagine hostile intentions
in others.[27] If a child bumps their chair, they assume it was intentional.
They adopt a blaming stance that affects their experience of social
interactions—what they attend to, how they make sense of it, and how
they manage their feelings, particularly their anger. Such children
develop a negative bias to their mind-reading narratives.[28] They don't
attend to relevant cues that might make for more accurate and more
positive imagined intentions. Consistent with their limited social imagination, they have difficulty generating productive solutions to social
problems and they show less self-regulation, often making impulsive
decisions.

Children who exhibit these difficulties are often viewed through a
fixed frame as having a "conduct disorder." However, children behaving
this way are more common in families where negative attributions are
common, and in communities marked by violence and disorder.[29] In
other words, when children learn to view the world as a hostile place,
they are predisposed to interpret others' actions as hostile and to place
blame. But this constellation of behaviors is not fixed. As we shall see
presently, it can be changed through instruction that is consistent with
what we have already considered.[30]

Talk and Social Imagination

Make no mistake, we teach social imagination, and language plays a big
role. In families, it is passed on through conversations that make connections between emotions and desires, particularly in causal explanations. For example, we say, "I can see why you would feel angry when
he took your toy. I wonder how he felt when you were playing with
toys and he didn't have one." In these conversations children learn how
to understand and share emotions and sensations—developing their
empathy—and expand their ability to understand the beliefs and
wishes in others.[31] Indeed, where these conversations are absent, such
as for many deaf preschool children raised by hearing parents, children
experience delays in development of social imagination, and their

development is similar to that of children with autism.[32] Even in the case of autism, though, where limited development of social imagination might be viewed as physiological,[33] instruction pays off. With modeling, role-play, performance feedback, and practice identifying emotions and beliefs, particularly false beliefs, even children with autism can be taught to mind read, and when they are, their social relationships also improve.[34]

Just having children talk about others through storytelling, as we saw with Jesse's class and *The Summer My Father Was Ten*, is a very good start.[35] Choosing books that have emotional tensions and conflicts and inviting conversation about feelings, motives, and beliefs is easy enough to get started. Use mental verbs. *What are you thinking? What am I thinking? What is he thinking? Imagine, feel, believe, wonder, want, like, need, know*, and so forth all invite conversations about what happens inside people's heads. So we ask questions like these: "Why do you think Mo Willems made the pigeon say that?"; "Do you think he believes him?"; "How do you think he feels about that?"; "What do you think he is trying to do?"; "Is he worried do you think?"; and "How can you tell?" Mental state words fall naturally into these conversations, and children's use of them expands along with their social imagination.[36] The hardest part for most of us is then keeping our mouths shut and not judging what children say.

I should say that these conversations are not limited to narrative texts. Conversations like this also occur around works of nonfiction. Science and history, no less than literacy, involve people, a fact that children must come to reckon with. Pegeen Jensen read *Snowflake Bentley*[37] with her students—a book about the first person to photograph snowflakes and recognize their uniqueness. Bentley encountered many failures along the way. Pegeen asked her students about a particular event, "How do you think he felt about that, as a scientist?" Differences in perspective also arise when we are engaging different explanatory theories in science and math.

Social Problem Solving

Helping children solve normal social problems is also a concrete cornerstone not only of building social imagination but also of classroom management and social life. One of Susie Althof's kindergartners, Dequan, comes to her with a problem. His chair at his table is bumping into the chair of the student at the next table so that he can't get into his seat. Susie asks him, "Did you already talk to the other person involved?" To which he nods his assent. "Oh," she says, "so that's why you need me?" He nods. They go to his chair and he shows her the problem. "Oohhh," she says, "so did you ask her to go to the other [empty] chair [around the other side of the table]?" This is met by a shake of the head, no. In a "silly you" voice, Susie responds, "Oh, so you forgot to talk to her about it. You don't need me. You forgot to talk to her. Use your words now."

> **Dequan:** A'isha, can you go sit at the other side (*of the table*)?
> **Susie:** Because . . .
> **Dequan:** Because, 'cause I can't get in my seat and I can't move.
> **Susie:** (*To A'isha.*) Do you remember whenever he comes over to that table you help him by moving to the other side? Remember that? Can you practice that? When he comes over here and your chairs bump each other then what can you do?
> **A'isha:** (*Describes strategy.*)
> **Susie:** Yeah. See how you two worked that out by yourselves? Dequan, you just had to explain to your partner what the problem was and why it was a problem. A'isha wants to help make the classroom a place where we can all learn together.

At no point in the exchange does Susie accuse or criticize. She does not mention that Dequan told her that he had spoken to A'isha when he hadn't. Only one lesson is necessary here. She arranges for them to talk productively to each other and offers a narrative of independence and interdependent learning. At the same time, she reminds them of their goal, making the classroom a place where we can all learn together. By insisting that the children express their needs, feelings, and their logic ("because . . ."), Susie helps them develop their social imagination further but also provides them with identities, frames, and strategies that will help them become more socially independent in the future.

As another example, during kindergarten class meeting, Susie addresses a problematic interaction that occurred during independent work time.

> **Susie:** We want to help each other be the best that we can be, alright? What else was going on? Eduardo, will you talk to me about what was going on with you and Denzel?
> (*Eduardo explains the problem.*)
> **Susie:** And how are you feeling about that, Denzel?

Denzel: Bad because he didn't help me to make the puzzle.
Susie: Did you ask him for help?
Denzel: (*Mumbles.*) No.
Susie: Ahhhh.
Several students: You have to ask him.
Susie: If you need help, what do we do?
Several students: (*Various versions of "ask them."*)
Susie: Because we can't read other people's minds, can we? No. If you ask for help then of course we're going to . . .
Students: Help.
Susie: Help you. So. You know what? Eduardo, come to the middle and just pretend like you're playing with something. Denzel, come to the middle and ask him for help.
Denzel: (*Very quiet request.*)
Susie: (*To Eduardo.*) And what do you say? Sure, I'll help you.
Eduardo: Sure I'll help you.
Susie: Try it again. Ask him again.
Denzel: Will you please help me?
Eduardo: Sure.
Susie: See how easy that was? Alright. Are we ready to get on with our day? Alright. Let's keep watching each other and noticing how it's going, okay? 'Cause it's your job to try to be the . . . best that you can be.
Students: Best that you can be.

Susie insists that the students articulate their problems and feelings. There is no accusation, only an assumption that people will run into problems, and that when they do they need to have strategies to solve them. When necessary, she helps them find the appropriate words to use.

Susie is helping her students build, and embody, social problem-solving routines that include using their social imagination to figure out how best to proceed, and to recognize what information their social partner will need. These practices are not unlike strategies advocated by Augusto Boal in *Theatre of the Oppressed*.[38] When oppressed people are used to being positioned poorly in social interactions, they role-play alternative scenarios and innovate in order to physically embody more productive interaction patterns.

As teachers, we increase our skill at social imagination the more we listen to children. Social imagination is our stock-in-trade. Noticing when a student doesn't understand, or when students are feeling cranky, is what makes it possible to anticipate and prevent problems. Imagining problems from students' perspectives allows us to teach. Teachers whose social imagination is well developed are likely to beget students with well developed social imaginations, not by magic, but by helping students listen to each other (enabling the teacher to listen in), make their thinking available, and imagine the thinking of others, and by constantly reminding the students of the significance of these practices.

Students Encountering the Most Difficulty

I described earlier the relationship between social imagination and behavior problems. It is probably hardest for us to apply what we know about teaching to the students who present us with the most difficulties, so it's important to be confident that doing so will bring results. In a series of three studies with elementary school minority students in high-risk neighborhoods, Cynthia Hudley and her colleagues developed an after-school program for the most aggressive and least motivated students.[39] Using pictures and role-play, Hudley and her colleagues taught these students how to more accurately judge people's feelings and motives—why people behave in particular ways—and how to distinguish between accidental and hostile acts. They also taught the students how to manage social problems, productively explain problematic events, and see the value of admitting responsibility, apologizing, and making amends—and to be more inclined to forgiveness when others apologize. On the academic front, they taught the students to take on realistic academic challenges, to make short-term goals, to attribute outcomes to effort rather than uncontrollable factors, and to focus on improvement. They taught them that asking for help is more successful when you have already tried to figure something out. In other words, their instruction directed the students toward a dynamic-learning frame, agency, accurate social imagination, and social problem-solving.

The students improved in their self-control at home and at school, they became more cooperative and persistent and less aggressive, and they improved academically. For students in control groups, none of this was true. Hudley and her colleagues point out that this was in spite of the fact that there were no positive models in the group and that it was an after-school program with no back-up during the regular school day. Imagine how effective these strategies are when teachers, like Susie, assume that this is a normal part of teaching during the school day.

Big Deal, No Problem

Developing social imagination is a big deal and should be a curricular goal. Even if teaching social imagination didn't register directly on state tests, there are compelling reasons to invest in it. To again be bluntly practical, classroom management depends substantially on children taking into account others' feelings and interests. Social imagination enables social decision making, and since learning, literacy, and inquiry are fundamentally social, we should approach teaching in ways that foster it.

Fortunately, teaching social imagination isn't that complicated. When Jesse's students discussed *The Summer My Father Was Ten*, consider how deeply they explored the emotions and motivational tensions in the two characters' minds, and in the process made available to others their own feelings and motives. Could there be a better demonstration (assessment) of children's social imagination—or a better experience for developing it? "What makes you think this is what Mr. Bellavista is thinking?" draws the children's attention to the signs and logic that form the basis of mind reading. And, of course, the teacher's excellent command of the language is shown in her consummate ability to keep her mouth shut while the children engage each other's views.[40]

CHAPTER 7

Moral Agency: Moral Development and Civic Engagement

I think in eighth grade before I ever had this [dialogic] class,

someone would say something and I would say . . . I would just not

even think about it, I would just say yes and take his side on it. But

this class, when it started up, I actually had an opinion of my own.

And I can state it without ever being scared or shy. So this class,

really, anytime I hear a new issue in the news or something like

that, I really like to think about it and get into all the facts and

details. I never used to do that before this class. Never.

—Eighth-grade student[1]

In recent years, along with complaints about test scores, there has been frequent lamenting about the lack of "character education" and "civic engagement." We mistakenly view these as subjects that compete with academics for valuable school time. But the dialogic instruction described in Chapter 5 not only advances academic achievement but also increases civic engagement as the opening student quote suggests.[2] Whether we like it or not, children are acquiring "character" and dispositions toward civic engagement (or not) as we teach them about history, literacy, math, and science. Their moral development doesn't just stop because we choose not to think about it.

Mary Cowhey gives considerable thought to this development in her wonderful book, *Black Ants and Buddhists*. For example, as part of the social studies curriculum, her first and second graders studied slavery. They discussed original documents, such as a letter sent by Benjamin Banneker, an African American mathematician, surveyor, and inventor, to Thomas Jefferson, in which Banneker eloquently pointed out the conflict between the Declaration of Independence and his ownership of slaves. They learned details not known to most adults, such as that Muslims at Ramadan, and Quakers too, as an act of charity, used to buy slaves their freedom. Months after this study, Mary explains, they were studying money in math, when a second grader, Thomas, suddenly initiated a discussion with this exclamation:

> *"Look at this! I can't believe it!" His tablemates leaned in to get a good look. "They put Jefferson's picture on the money! He got a nickel!"*
> *"So?" a first grader asks. "All the money gots guys on it."*
> *Thomas stood up and said, "But this guy said all men were created equal, and he owned slaves!" After a quick discussion at his table, Thomas and company decided they should protest this. Clearly there'd been an error. Thomas wrote a letter to the U.S. Treasury informing them that Presidents Jefferson and Washington had been slave owners and should be taken off the money for that reason. He suggested replacing them with other heroes such as Frederick Douglass, Sojourner Truth, Lucretia Mott, and Benjamin Banneker.*[3]

I want my children and their children in a class like this.

Fairness and Difference

The money example is not a rare incident in Mary's class. These children are actively on the lookout for injustice. When they see it, they announce it: "That's not right." Their thinking quickly proceeds to "I'd better do something." They don't just have a strong moral compass; they have the moral engine to go with it. A sign on the wall quoting the Dalai Lama captures this spirit: "It is not enough to be compassionate. You must act." The sign is a good touchstone, but there is a great deal more in the daily conversation that goes into the development of this strong sense of moral agency.

Morals are largely normative. We learn what to attend to and what to ignore—what to value—and how to act. What we choose to discuss with children and how we discuss it shapes these norms. Mary considers this when she chooses what to place in her morning message. For example, shortly after Barack Obama took office, he signed his first bill, the Lilly Ledbetter Fair Pay Act. Lilly Ledbetter discovered that for nineteen years she had been paid far less than men doing the same job but that she could do nothing about it because more than 180 days had passed since the first discriminatory pay event. The company Lilly worked for required workers not to discuss their pay, so she didn't make the discovery until too late. The new law made it possible for people like Lilly to sue the company for discrimination. Mary's morning message to her second graders described the law in simple language. She personalized the historical moment by showing a press photo of Obama signing the law with Lilly in the picture. She then asked the children for comments. She asked whether it was fair or not fair.

But fairness, they learn, is not simple. One child, searching for an explanation, suggested that, like one of the children in the class, maybe Ledbetter had too many bleeding noses and couldn't work so much. Mary responded to this, as to other questions, by taking it seriously and without judgment. "Not as I understand it, but that raises another question. What if someone is more sick? Should they get paid less?" This prompted a deeply philosophical conversation about equity.

Routinely raising for discussion issues of fairness in the world and in the classroom establishes a norm: It is something that we care about in this community. Mary does not take a position on these issues; she only raises them for discussion. By routinely having the discussions, though, of "Is that fair?" she establishes that, in this community, fairness is important. Students become aware that people will differ on what fairness means in any given case. Even if there is no agreement, as students construct their own view they will engage multiple perspectives, building their social imaginations and helping them de-center—building the capacity to act for fairness, even when it conflicts with other personal desires.

There is still more to be done though. If children are to think more broadly about these issues and actually remember them, they have to make links to other things they know about. To build these links, Mary might ask, "Does this connect to any other things you have encountered?" In the discussion about Lilly Ledbetter, however, she didn't have to. The press photograph showed eight white people and two African Americans (including Obama), and a child linked the equity problem to African Americans. Mary said, "Say more about that," and the student explained that it was like equal pay regardless of race.

On another occasion, Mary might explore the concept of equity into other areas and ask how the examples are and are not like the equal pay issue. This time she simply moved on with "Thanks for noticing that," but the extension to equity and race played an important role beyond helping the children to generalize and remember. It increased their moral reach—the breadth of individuals to whom our moral commitments extend. For example, there have been times when perfectly good societal moral commitments did not extend to women or to African Americans. In recent years in the United States, we have wrestled with whether our moral commitments extend to illegal immigrants, to prisoners, to gay people, or to people in other countries. This is complex learning. It has a lot to do with how we think about difference and how often we practice extending our empathy to those who are beyond our experience. And we're back again to social imagination.

Culture, Stereotype, and Prejudice

Moral development and social imagination are closely intertwined, and there is considerable cross-cultural commonality. For example, having Chinese preschoolers talk about characters and other people through storytelling improves their social imaginations just as it does for American children.[4] There are, however, cultural differences in social logic that we must attend to as we develop our social imaginations. If we are to prepare children for a multicultural or global society, we will need to learn more about cultural differences in social reasoning. For example, in the United States mainstream, issues to do with caring for friends, family, and others are matters of personal choice. You don't have to do it, particularly if you are not close to them or don't agree with them. In some cultures, however, such as India, these are moral matters—matters of duty—and the extent to which a person is relationally close or shares interests is less relevant.[5] Such differences will complicate social imagination, because imagining motives and feelings will need to take these differences into account.

As a related example, there are also differences in the meaning of duty. For mainstream Americans, duties are obligations. They are experienced as burdens because they limit personal choice. They are endured, not enjoyed.[6] In more collectivist societies, such as India, or Native American culture, duty is exactly what a person aspires to and is thus quite satisfying.[7] When people from India were asked about times when they helped a friend when it was expected and when it was not, they experienced both situations as freely chosen. Mainstream Americans experienced the two events differently. They only felt they had freely chosen when there was no expectation. They felt compelled to help when it was expected. Cross-cultural social imagination is more difficult, but is becoming increasingly important. The value of diversity in our classrooms, along with conversations that maximize the value of that diversity for intellectual, social, and moral development, can't be overstated.

We also have to talk about other sorts of difference. One day, in celebration of Langston Hughes's birthday, Mary and her class read the photo-illustrated version of his poem "My People." A student remarked, "They're not really his people. He doesn't own them."

Without judging the comment, Mary asked, "Why do you think he says that?" After hearing some responses, she asked, "'Black people,' is that more than his family?"

After a moment's thought, the students responded, "Yes."

"If he said 'African American,' would that be more?" Each question drew new realizations. They were engaged in analytic logic, a branch of philosophy (and math) which itself is intellectually stimulating. In the moral sphere, she was helping them think about similarity, difference, and inclusion. She reminded them about their recent study of melanin and then observed, "I like how Langston Hughes included in the poem everyone from babies to old people."

Since skin color is still on the conversational table, a student confessed, "My skin is darker than my mom's."

Knowing his background, Mary asked, "And where did you get that from?"

"My dad."

"Yes, because he's from India and that's near the equator."

Continually increasing awareness of difference is a way of breaking down stereotype.[8] Stereotype is a result of arbitrarily restricting the examination of difference. Once we get past the obvious surface features of people, such as skin color and gender, and attend to interests, food tastes, musical preference, and so forth, we start seeing that all stereotypes break down, and we become increasingly aware both of diversity and of similarity, which expands the children's moral community. It reduces the number of people who they might otherwise exclude from their moral responsibilities.[9] Perspective taking—mentally walking in another's mind—is a very effective way of reducing prejudice, because we can see more of ourselves in the other and the other in ourselves.[10]

Stereotype and prejudice are not things most people overtly espouse, yet human beings are predisposed to stereotype as a sort of intellectual efficiency. It is a "natural" tendency that citizenship requires outgrowing if we aspire to a just society. You might think it has nothing to do with academic performance, but it does. Margaret Shih and Adam Pittinsky gave a group of Asian women a math test.[11] But first they gave some of them a survey. Some took a survey that subtly emphasized their femaleness with questions like "Do you prefer single-sex dorms or co-ed dorms?" For another group the survey emphasized their Asian-ness. A third group took no survey. When they took the math test, those whose attention was drawn to their Asian-ness performed better than those who took no survey. Those whose attention was drawn to their femaleness did worse. Repeating the experiment with a language test instead of a math test, the order of performance was reversed. In each case, their performance was influenced by the identity they took up through the associated stereotype. The same effects have been shown in five- to seven-year-old girls and eleven- to thirteen-year-old girls.[12] Similarly, all it takes to make very capable African American undergraduates perform badly on a test is to have them fill out a demographic item that identifies them as African American before they take the test.[13] The effects can be reduced by interventions that invite participants to take up a dynamic theory.[14]

Threat of stereotype is particularly powerful within a fixed frame, such as when students believe a test can determine how much ability they have. When Armand Chatard and his colleagues introduced a test to high school students as "a test of whether there are differences in intellectual performance between children from African and European parents," students who were more inclined to stereotype and prejudice performed according to their stereotype.[15] However, when Chatard reduced the fixed-performance orientation by introducing the test as simply "a test of individual differences," that didn't happen. Again, the way we frame classroom activities influences what students think they're doing and who they think they are.

You might think it a good idea to eliminate negative stereotypes but keep the positive ones, but even positive stereotypes have their downside. Aside from the fact that it can be quite stressful to live up to the stereotype even if it is an identity one wishes to take up, we have to remember that a fixed frame is a fixed frame.

Social Reasoning, Caring,
and Social Action

In response to an annoying behavioral transgression, fourth-grade teacher Jeralyn Johnson said, "That's distracting to me, so would you please stop?" She didn't just say, "Stop that!" What's the difference? The latter response, framed as a command, relies on positional authority, the teacher's power over the student. By complying, the student publicly recognizes his or her (and other students') subordinate position. By contrast, the teacher's response framed as a request with a logic emphasizing the consequences for others, offers a more symmetrical relationship. While not eliminating the teacher's authority, it offers a moral choice that relies less on subordination. At the same time, it publicly announces that it is okay for people to make requests of other community members based on the consequences of their behavior. Furthermore, it offers a model for how to do it— by explaining your logic. As with most other aspects of apprenticeships, modeling productive social behavior is useful, but it is most effective when accompanied by our logic, and it is particularly effective when that logic emphasizes the effects on other people.[16]

This is also true with discipline. Discipline that foregrounds the emotional consequences of a behavior or intended behavior expands both children's levels of sympathy and their prosocial behavior.[17] For example, rather than saying "Don't lean back in your chair like that," Jeralyn Johnson added, "because I care too much to see you get hurt." The logic strengthens the relationship that is the basis for the student's compliance, and when teachers are seen as caring, students are socially and academically more motivated.[18] At the same time, Jeralyn's comment models and reinforces important classroom values, caring for others, and taking responsibility for behavior, and the comment invokes echoes of classroom conversations that invite social imagination and caring.

An ethic of caring is also evident in Susie Althof's kindergarten. One day, Susie is going to put on the word wall a word her kindergarten class agrees it has mastered. Sometimes doing this requires her to stand on her chair. Anticipating this, Qadir says, "Be careful." Susie hears him and says, "Thank you, Qadir, for caring about the people in your life. Your mother is so lucky to have you—caring about people." Although this sounds like praise, it is not. She says, "Thank you," recognizing Qadir's contribution as a gift, and at the same time providing a useful narrative for him to live into. In the same way, discipline that points out the consequence of prosocial behavior and attributes a motive of kindness and generosity is likely to be most effective.[19] Parenting that provides a supportive environment and engages children in thinking about moral problems, providing explanations and suggestions, is the most appropriate course of action for parents. Teaching in school is no different.

These matters are not simply about classroom management. They are about the kinds of moral agency we wish to see in society. Samuel and Pearl Oliner studied people who chose to help or not help Jews in Nazi Germany.[20] In interviews, they found that rescuers acquired their sense of generosity from influential adults, such as their parents, both from their modeling and from explicit statements. These parents were more likely to use causal statements in their discipline and to stress that their moral responsibility was to everyone, and they demonstrated as much. The families had closer relationships with one another than did those who did not help Jews. Inconsiderate, uncaring behavior in these families was grounds for discipline, but it was discipline with reason.

Authoritarian and punitive discipline, it turns out, can undermine the development of conscience, sympathy, and prosocial behavior while offering a problematic model for the child. Although it seems perverse, rewarding prosocial behavior is not so different from punitive discipline. It is part of the same conversation. Second and fifth graders who thought they would be rewarded for helping hospitalized children were more inclined to help, but subsequently when they did not expect rewards, they were less inclined to help. In other words, rewards can increase prosocial behavior in the short term, but children who are persistently motivated by rewards appear less motivated to help when the rewards are not there.[21]

The Long Term

Perhaps you think I am looking at too big a picture—that schooling doesn't or shouldn't have such extensive reach. Consider, then, the work of Lawrence Schweinhart and David Weikart.[22] In 1997, they reported on a direct comparison of different preschool programs over the long haul. Three- and four-year-old children living in poverty had been randomly assigned to different preschool programs and followed until the age of twenty-three. Each program was two and a half hours each day and had biweekly home visits that amplified the effects of the program.

One program, Direct Instruction, was in the behaviorist tradition: scripted, teacher-directed, closely sequenced, and focused on academic goals. Behavior management was based on systematic reward and punishment. The High/Scope program was in the constructivist and cognitive-developmental traditions and emphasized collaborative planning by teacher and students. It included a plan-do-review cycle that put children in control of their learning and had them reflect on the consequences of their choices and actions. The program attended to academics more broadly defined than in the Direct Instruction program, but it also specifically addressed approaches to learning, social and emotional issues, and health and well-being. It included helping children address social conflicts through problem solving.

This latter aspect of the program is particularly consistent with the research I have described so far in this chapter. For example, social problem solving continues to be a core element in the High/Scope curriculum. It involves first acknowledging the children's feelings, then gathering information about the nature of the problem, not asking the reason for it. So you would ask "What's the problem?" rather than "Why did you hit him?" Asking for a description of the problem gives a little psychological distance, whereas asking why will get narrative responses, including problematic attributions that we don't want to have on the table. Next, you would restate the problem so that the children can focus on something that they agree on, that is amenable to solution, and that is not personalized. With a clear problem, you can ask "How could we solve this problem?" and offer possibilities if necessary. Finally, you can offer an agentive narrative: "You solved that problem. You figured out what the problem was and you worked out a solution."

There were no differences between these programs in academic performance (at least on tests). That is not to say that there were no effects. Indeed, the outcomes of the study strongly favor the High/Scope preschool students, particularly in terms of their relational and moral agency (see Figure 7.1). These are not trivial outcomes, and a similar study following children through age twenty-seven arrived at similar conclusions.[23] Schweinhart and his colleagues argue that these benefits amount to a return of about $7.16 on each dollar spent on the preschool education.[24] Indeed, a follow-up study of High/Scope students versus those not in the program to age forty showed that High/Scope children achieved higher levels of schooling, with 20 percent more graduating from high school, 14 percent more employed, and mean annual earnings 36 percent higher.[25] The crime rates were again significantly different, and the researchers estimate that the

Figure 7.1 Comparison of Significant Outcomes of Direct Instruction and High/Scope Preschool Programs Through Age Twenty-Three.

Indicator of Social-Moral Development	Percentage of Students	
	High/Scope	Direct Instruction
Treated for emotional impairment or disturbance during schooling	6	47
Engaged at some point in volunteer work	43	11
Arrested for a felony	10	39
Arrested for a property crime	0	38
Reported that various people gave them a hard time	36	69
Married and living with spouses	31	0

return to the public in constant dollars was $12.90 for every dollar invested in the program.[26] Of course, that is on top of the benefits to the individuals themselves and those who live and interact with them.

You might be skeptical about such studies since there are many variables between preschool and forty years of age. Remember, however, the students were randomly assigned to the program and subsequent life events were also randomly distributed—except to the extent that that the students' behavior changed the likelihood of events. I take some comfort in the fact that the findings are consistent with the shorter-term experimental research I have mentioned throughout this book. If an intervention changes a child's social imagination, he is likely to choose different subsequent courses of action and construct different relationships, which in turn would affect subsequent choices and relationships. Such interventions change a child's trajectory. There is no doubt that long-term studies such as these are too rare. However, as an evaluation of schooling practices, these indicators are no less significant than the rather trivial academic tests we currently use.

Taking Moral Development Seriously

Whether we like to think about it or not, while we are teaching math or science or language arts, we are also nurturing particular forms of moral development. Pretending otherwise will not change the evidence or serve children or society well. Taking moral development seriously would require adjustments similar to those we have considered in other chapters, such as developing children's social imaginations, but one shift is probably central. We tend to view conflicts in the classroom as simply distractions from academic learning, so we try to eliminate them as quickly as possible by invoking our authority as teachers. This might get us back to academics more quickly, but at the cost of reducing the moral authority and commitment of the students. It might be better to view these interruptions as opportunities for building a moral compass and both the tools and the inclination for social problem solving. Unfortunately, the more high-stakes testing pressure is applied to teachers, the more authoritarian they become and the less inclined they will be to invest time in social problem-solving.[27]

Besides, confronting conflict is not easy. Most of us have not been prepared to talk through conflict with others, which makes it hard for us to model or to scaffold for our students. But conflicts are opportunities to examine our assumptions and values and they are exactly the places where students find morality most engaging. Social problems offer concrete spaces for understanding different perspectives, understanding and managing emotions, learning strategies for negotiating social conflict, and asserting a commitment to fairness. Conflicts offer opportunities to make clear that we value considerate, empathic behavior and disapprove of nonconsiderate behavior, making causal links to emotional consequences. We capitalize on these opportunities often in order to emphasize that it is normal to encounter and collaboratively resolve conflicts and to manage our emotions and language and consider others' feelings in order to do so. Sometimes we point out inconsiderate choices and their consequences, showing that they are not normally accepted.

It isn't easy for students to take up this way of thinking and acting. Even grown-ups can be exposed to ridicule for revealing their empathy, and ridicule can crush efforts toward equity. For example, early efforts to make language more equitable were stopped cold by ridicule using the term *politically correct*. Designed by those who were uncomfortable with changing their language, or perhaps comfortable with the social structures from which they benefited, the term was particularly effective.

Consequently, we want to show students how to resist the influence of others who make fun of their empathic feelings, help them to figure considerateness into their choice of friends, and help them to make the decision to be kind and courageous people. We have to recognize, however, that this is not straightforward for students in economically distressed urban settings, because often in those communities there is a certain survival value to aggressiveness; our conversations with such students should not pretend otherwise.[28] Our conversations can, however, help students to recognize contexts in which different strategies might be most productive, and the benefits of the practices we offer in the classroom.

Just as there is no sense pretending that we can teach academic subjects without teaching moral development, there is no sense pretending that there is universal agreement on a moral code to develop. Perhaps, though, we might agree that we would like children to develop as mentally healthy moral agents—people who have a sense of their moral commitments and stand up for them, do not assume in others the same set of commitments, but assume that differences should be negotiated equitably. These are threads that we are morally bound to weave into classroom life. They are a foundation for democratic living.

CHAPTER 8

Thinking Together, Working Together

In the long history of humankind (and animal kind, too) those who learned to collaborate and improvise most effectively have prevailed.
— CHARLES DARWIN[1]

Our main advantage as human beings lies in our ability to think together. Individually we wouldn't be at the top of the food chain. We are quite vulnerable to predators with keener senses, better camouflage, greater speed, and aerial and aquatic mobility. When it comes to sheer muscle, with some notable exceptions, we are relatively puny. Fortunately, we have some important advantages. We are gregarious, we have language, and we can think. Together, these give us strength in numbers and the possibility of specialization. Specialization only works because of our ability to think and to coordinate goals and actions through language. Ultimately, though, these gifts open the possibility of bringing multiple minds to a problem, potentially allowing us to solve problems that would stump the individual mind. However, my experiences with committee meetings and politicians suggest that, as a society, we have yet to reach our peak in capitalizing on this potential advantage.

In spite of considerable research on the effectiveness of collaborative learning, as a society we have not taken seriously the extraordinary significance and potential of this gift.[2] We continue to view children solely in terms of their individual academic development and the individual cognitive processes they will need to succeed on individual tests. We conveniently forget that children's ability to use language as a tool for thinking on their own has its origins in thinking together.[3] We also forget that most problems of any significance require the application of more than one mind. The question is, can children learn to use, say, three minds together to accomplish things that the three minds separately could not?

With that question in mind, consider the following examples of thirteen- to fourteen-year-olds trying to solve a nonverbal reasoning problem from an IQ test together.[4] The problem requires deciding which of eight options is the missing piece to a puzzle. The puzzle has three rows and three columns of patterned pieces that vary in complex but systematic ways. To solve the problem you have to figure out the system. For example, from row to row or column to column an element of the pattern might rotate 90 degrees or systematically gain or lose features, a background might change, a sequence might begin at different points, and so forth. Tess, Graham, and Suzie are looking at the pattern in problem D9 and pointing to options:

Example 1
Tess: It's that.
Graham: It's that, 2.
Tess: 2 is there.
Graham: It's 2.
Tess: 2 is there.
Graham: What number do you want then?
Tess: It's that because there ain't two of them.
Graham: It's number 2, look one, two.
Tess: I can count, are we all in agreement on it?
Suzie: (Circles number 2 on the answer sheet) No.
Graham: Oh, after she's circled it![5]

Are we having fun yet? It is not hard to see the problems with their interaction, and choosing the wrong alternative, which they do, is not the main one. In this interaction, each is trying to be right. They are individually trying to solve the problem correctly in the presence of others. They are not using others to help them solve the problem. Indeed, they have turned their disagreement into a relational conflict, as happens in a performance frame (see Chapter 2).[6] On the positive side, Tess offers a modest explanation and checks that they all agree.

However, the thinking behind their choices is unavailable and Suzie is excluded, or excludes herself, from the process.

Example 2
Suzie: D9 now, that's a bit complicated it's got to be . . .
Graham: A line like that, a line like that and it ain't got a line with that.
Tess: It's got to be that one.
Graham: It's going to be that don't you think? Because look all the rest have got a line like that and like that, I think it's going to be that because . . .
Tess: I think it's number 6.
Suzie: No I think it's number 1.
Graham: Wait no, we've got number 6, wait stop, do you agree that it's number 1? Because look that one there is blank, that one there has got them, that one there has to be number 1, because that is the one like that. Yes. Do you agree?
(Tess nods in agreement)
Suzie: D9 number 1.
(Suzie writes '1', which is the correct answer).[7]

This second example is quite different from the first. Although they are solving the same problem, the youngsters are actually engaged in a different activity. They are trying to solve a problem together, not individually trying to be right. They make more of their thinking available for the others to use. Their explanations are longer, and often prefaced with "I think . . . ," which allows for the possibility of difference and uncertainty. The difference in relational tone is at least as important. As we have seen in earlier chapters, the children are not only learning how to think together but also learning how to think about and to treat others. If group members were to give an estimation of the competence of their teammates on the two different occasions, they would be more positive in the second example.[8]

What makes these two examples fascinating is that they are the same group of children attempting to solve the same problem before and after learning how to think together. These examples were taken from a study by Neil Mercer and his colleagues. In their study, the children took the nonverbal reasoning test in groups of three, and then they took a different form of the test individually. Three months later, they took the tests again in groups and as individuals. In the meantime, half of them had been taught how to think together. As you would expect based on the preceding transcripts, the children who had learned how to think together became more successful on the test in the group situation—their group IQ increased. In addition, when they subsequently took another version of the IQ test individually, the children who had learned to think together outperformed those who had not. In other words, the experience of thinking together productively in a mixed-ability group actually increased the individual children's measured intelligence.

This study illustrates several important points. First, a group can have intelligence that can be more (or less) than the sum of its members' intelligence. Second, what makes a group's intelligence greater than the sum of the individual intelligences is learnable. It turns out that the collective intelligence of a group is not particularly related to the average, or maximum, intelligence of individuals in the group.[9] However, group intelligence is related to some other factors we are familiar with from Chapters 5 and 6—the average social sensitivity of the group and how evenly the group distributes conversational turns. Group intelligence also turns out to be related to the proportion of the group members who are female; however, that is entirely about the social sensitivity they bring, and we know that can be learned.

In other words, the effectiveness of multiple minds depends somewhat on the capabilities of the individual minds involved, though not in the ways we have historically imagined. But it is equally true that our ability to think alone is substantially dependent on our ability to think together. Individual minds are nurtured in the conversations—the interactive thinking—of the community. Thinking well together leads to thinking well alone. But by thinking together, I don't mean just the rational logic of the conversations. The emotional and relational support we provide for each other in the process of thinking together is equally important for the development of individual minds.

The study also shows that intelligence, as measured by a "non-verbal," "culture-fair" IQ test, can be changed by the history of verbal interactions in the group. This might surprise people who have adopted a fixed frame. People who adopt a fixed frame often complain that in collaborative learning, the smart children are wasting their time "teaching" their less endowed peers. As this study shows, that is not the case. In other words, even if we (foolishly) persisted with our individualistic view of development, we could justify teaching children how to think together both because of its effects on individual students and because even the most capable students can do more together when they know how.

Research shows the effects of collaborative learning like this are consistently positive and not constrained to problem solving and literacy. The same consequences have been documented in science and in math.[10] Indeed, what I find most compelling is the breadth of the effects. Learning to think together doesn't just impact achievement in a subject area. Rather, it affects the whole child and his relationships to himself and others. Various experimental studies reviewed by Steve Trickey and Keith Topping have shown that, compared with control groups, children taught how to think together show an increase in the following:[11]

- Reasoning ability
- Comprehension
- Expressive language
- Creative thinking
- Examining assumptions
- Willingness to speak in public
- Willingness to listen to and consider others' ideas
- Frequency of providing reasons or evidence for their view
- Quality of interpersonal relationships
- Confidence, self-esteem, and persistence
- Supportive group interactions

Some of the interventions showing these effects have children thinking together for only an hour per week,[12] yet the effects persist over time.[13]

I hope these outcomes, which are consistent across a range of age levels, convince you that teaching children how to think together is important. None of these outcomes is trivial, and collectively they remind us that there is more to teaching, and to education, than improving test scores. Nonetheless, if you wanted to make an argument for instructional efficiency, remember that these gains are generated mostly when the teacher is not even with the students.

Even if these outcomes had not been established, we should still teach children how to think together, because most problems of substance aren't amenable to solution by individual minds; they need the force of multiple minds, in part because, as Einstein pointed out, "No problem can be solved from the same level of consciousness that created it." However, as we saw in the first of the two transcripts, merely bringing multiple minds to a problem doesn't guarantee more effective problem solving. In fact, prior to learning how to think together, the group performance on the nonverbal reasoning test was not even as good as the average of individual performances. Perhaps this reminds you of some of the committees you have served on, or the United States Congress. However, even mediocre committees experience some successful problem solving, and Mercer and his colleagues examined how talk leading to successful problem solving is different from talk leading to unsuccessful problem solving. From previous chapters you could predict what they found. The successful items included more long turns (11 vs. 0) and more frequent use of "I think" (24 vs. 1), "I agree" (18 vs. 3), and "because" (26 vs. 6).[14] In other words, when groups took their time to explain their logic and to make it available for others to work with, they were successful.

When children are thinking together, they generate strategies, and the strategies become available for others to use. Dong Ting and her colleagues, for example, studied children's use of argumentation strategies when discussing books.[15] They deliberately chose stories that contained moral dilemmas, such as *Doctor De Soto*, *The Paper Bag Princess*, and *Ronald Morgan Goes to Bat*, so that children would take up positions and argue their cases—thinking together, using their different perspectives to understand the story better.[16]

In these discussions, children generated argumentation strategies of these forms:

- I think [POSITION], because [REASON].
- In the story, it says [EVIDENCE].
- If [ACTION], then [BAD CONSEQUENCE].
- What if [SCENARIO]?
- But [COUNTERARGUMENT].
- Let [CLASSMATE] talk!
- Put [CLASSMATE] in [SCENARIO].
- What do you think, [CLASSMATE]?

The students' use of these strategies, and others, grew like a snowball. Once a strategy was used once in the discussion, the probability that it would be used a second time was 88 percent, and if the strategy was used a second time there was a 90 percent chance it would be used a third time. The strategies were also used with increasing speed. It took about six minutes on average for any particular strategy to be used the first time, but once it had been used, the second use occurred in about three minutes and the third in little over a minute and a half. And it wasn't just the same student using the strategy. The use of the strategy spread. Looking across all the discussion groups, by the time a strategy appeared in the conversation six times it was being used by nearly half of the students. By the time it was used eight or more times, it was being used by over two-thirds of the students. They were individually acquiring the thinking that the group was doing together, and when they wrote essays, the strategies showed up in their writing.

Other researchers have found the same thing. For example, Heather Lattimer found that after longer discussions, eighth-grade students' journal responses were two and a half times more likely to provide evidence from a new data source, connections to other readings or prior knowledge, or to offer multiple interpretations than they were after a short discussion.[17] As one student explained:

> *You definitely have to have evidence to back you up. You can't just come in there with like just commentary and say how you feel and then expect to have people agree with you. Because what we are learning about, emotion is strong, but you can't just go in there with emotion, you have to go in there with evidence and quotes and statistics and stuff. You can't just say I feel this way, you know, and expect to have people listen to you . . . To be taken seriously in this class, you have to have a lot of evidence to back you up more.*

Children who have learned to think together in dialogic groups learn to take each other, and thus themselves, seriously. Students learn to listen to and find each other interesting, and these become properties of the learning community.

Generating these conversations is not that difficult. In fact, I use Ting Dong and her colleagues' study as an example partly because the students were Chinese and Korean fourth graders whose cultural experience in school was thoroughly monologic, with the teacher asking the questions and the students standing to respond individually or the class responding in unison. However, the students very quickly adapted. For example, in Ma Anshan, China, with an introduction that took only one minute and forty seconds, the students became engaged in dialogic interaction. It took them only one minute to stop looking at the researcher for confirmation, and their first discussion lasted over half an hour. The researcher's introduction did not assign roles to different students; it only asked them to listen to each other, take each other seriously, and hear all voices.[18]

Listening and Power

Mary Cowhey observes that the real test of a dialogic classroom is "to have the least-empowered children, the least articulate, take a leading role in that dialog while the more articulate children thoughtfully listen and consider things from their classmates' perspectives before they comment or question."[19] Perhaps it seems trivial to mention this, but in order to have dialogue, people have to listen to one another. I mention this because really listening to a partner is less common than it might seem, and because there is listening and then there is *listening*. Listening because you are interested is quite different from listening as a matter of vigilance or responsibility.[20] The more children come to appreciate each other as interesting and as sources of learning, the less they need vigilant listening, which is exhausting rather than enlivening.

The first step, then, is to arrange for children to be interesting to each other. This requires enabling them to bring their interests, experiences, and perspectives to their work. For example, when children are able to choose their own subject to write about, or choose their own way into writing about a particular topic, they will have more to say and they will say it in a way that others will find engaging to listen to. It will also help if they can be reasonably articulate.

When Jeralyn Johnson was discussing with her students a book she had just read with them, one of the students asked, "Could we do a summary?"

"Okay," she said. "Take ten silent seconds to think in your head, what could be the main idea of the story—and you need to support your main idea." Ten seconds later she said, "Okay, turn and talk with your partner and see what you can come up with together." This generated a lively discussion in which the children were fully engaged in speaking and listening—because they were interested and prepared. It helped, too, that although Jeralyn said "the main idea," which might have pointed toward certainty and a fixed frame, she prefaced it with "could be" and referred to "your main idea" to reduce the press for certainty. At the same time, she pushed them to take responsibility for their position by providing supporting evidence.

To help children become adept at listening, we can set a goal for them to learn their partner's view on an issue. We can ask first how they will find out what their partner is thinking and what they will do when they don't fully understand. Then we monitor, remind them, and show them both how to listen and the benefits of doing so. Sometimes for kindergartners (as well as politicians and other adults) this is difficult. The following interaction took place in Susie Althof's kindergarten class.

Susie: I'm wondering if you can share what your partner just said. Hmm. What your partner just said. Shatara, what did Janaya just say?

Shatara: She said that we didn't [unclear] and we had a great day.

Susie: Hmm. Is that what you said? (*Janaya nods.*) Your partner was listening to you. Isn't that awesome? What did your partner say, James?

James: No, I said it.

Susie: No, I'm asking you to tell me what your partner said.

James: He, . . . but I . . .

Susie: Too bad, so sad. I'm asking for what your partner said. Mario, can you tell me what Qadir said? (*Mario nods.*) What did Qadir say? He's listening to see if you were reeeally listening. Look at him, look, see how he's smiling? What did Qadir say?

Mario: [unclear]

Susie: Is that what you said, Qadir? Aaaah, you better whisper it and tell him again. Who can tell me what their partner said? I tricked you didn't I?

(*Conversation briefly pursues an important sidebar, then proceeds.*)

Susie: I want to hear what Denzel said.

Mario: That it was kind of noisy, just a little bit, but it was okay.

Susie: It was okay? Is that what you said? (*Denzel nods.*) Your partner was listening to you. Isn't it cool when you really listen to what your partner says? 'Cause your partner has fantastic ideas, don't they?

Even with practice, sometimes students forget and approach the conversation as simply a place to hear their own voice. For example, in Don Reed's fourth-grade class, Melinda and Anthony are engaged in partner talk about a book.[21] They have written sticky notes recording their thinking to prepare for their conversation. However, as Don joins them, Anthony is explaining to Melinda what is on his sticky note. Melinda waits until he has read his sticky note, and then begins reporting what she has on hers. Don intervenes, saying, "Hold on, Melinda, did you really listen to what Anthony said?"

Melinda responds by trying to repeat what he said: "He said that he wrote that . . . about the panther book? What did you say?"

Because of her realization that she has no idea what he said, she asks for clarification. Anthony explains his point, which is that the book is very like another book in its lyrical style of writing. Understanding this, which she had not previously noticed, she tries to remember the name for this sort of writing. When Don asks why they think the author chose the lyrical form, Anthony shrugs, but Melinda decides the form is calming and helps present the panther in a less scary light. Before he leaves them to continue their conversation, Don observes, "So, Melinda, you really listened to Anthony's idea, and the two of you stayed focused on it and talked more about it. Now you both understand something about this text and what the author is doing that you didn't understand before. Melinda, you had a sticky note to talk about, too. Anthony, be ready to really listen to Melinda's idea."

Don's transition comment accomplishes several important things. First, by ignoring Melinda's initial error, and focusing on her second, more successful listening attempt, he offers a productive narrative of the experience. Second, it is an agentive narrative for both students, because Don has made a causal link between the act of listening and their subsequent advance in understanding. Having offered them this productive narrative, he then invites them to rehearse it again independently by reminding them of their symmetrical, reciprocal roles and the centrality of listening.

Without Don's comments, the children would probably have had an unsuccessful experience discussing the text. Even if their experience had been successful, they would not have learned how to repeat it, or necessarily have been motivated to do so. Once children understand the personal and community benefits of listening, and how to do it, they will find it increasingly easy. In the process, they are likely to expand their social imaginations, to be less likely to take up a fixed frame with respect to knowledge, and to decrease their need for closure.

When each person in the classroom community is viewed as able to contribute to the development of knowledge, there is not the typical classroom hierarchy of those who have knowledge, usually the teachers, followed by the "top" students, down to those who don't have knowledge. Fostering more egalitarian relationships through collaborative talk emphasizes the class's work together and the value of each member of the classroom community in creating knowledge.

Listening is the foundation of a conversation and it requires that we are open to the possibility of changing our thinking. A turn-and-talk is not simply an opportunity to say what you have to say and allow someone else to do the same. When we are listening to a partner, we are actually doing more than that. We are offering through our bodies a responsiveness to the other that, in a sense, brings the other into being. If there is no responsiveness between us, no openness to being influenced by the other, there is no trust. It is through persistently being heard that we take ourselves seriously and view ourselves as agentive—someone who has interests and plans and acts accordingly.

Trust is an implicit part of listening, and both are foundational for group work.

Helping Children to Manage Thinking Together

Beyond listening, thinking together involves beliefs and expectations that we have explored in previous chapters. For example, we expect to have more interesting and powerful conversations when people bring different perspectives and when they disagree. However, disagreement only leads to better learning when we have learning goals, not when we have performance goals.[22] So everything we have learned about maintaining dialogic learning conversations is relevant for thinking together. In addition, we want children to notice how other people's thoughts stimulate their own thinking.

The first order of business is arranging for children to have the experience of thinking together. This experience can be prompted by anything from an evocative picture, to a book, a classroom or community concern, a math problem, scientific inquiry, or a news event. As Jesse Harrison showed us on pages 68–69 as she orchestrated class discussion of *The Summer My Father Was Ten*, it helps to have students turn and talk to a partner briefly to clarify their thoughts. We can look for opportunities to ensure that children who do not contribute frequently successfully do so by listening in on their turn and talks to know when they are well prepared and to set up the others to listen carefully to what they have to say. In the beginning we need to make sure that children understand that "turn and talk" doesn't mean merely turn and talk; it means building a conversation. Building a conversation means building on each other's ideas. Different ideas are good, but just as when we are reading, not all ideas that spring to mind help us with the current task. Sometimes we have to ask students to hold on to, or "park," their ideas while we "dig in" to another idea. When we do so, it's really important to say why and to remember to return, either publically or privately, to recognize the thinking that was parked.

Showing the children how they have built on or otherwise contributed to the group's thinking is important. We might say, "John, when you pushed back against our thinking, it showed us that we were making some unnecessary assumptions. You really helped us think more clearly about it. Then Erica was able to come up with a better solution to the problem." This helps children develop a sense of what they are doing—building ideas bigger—and how they are doing it—by adding ideas. In the process, they gain a sense of agency.

For children to think together productively, they have to understand the rules of thinking engagements and to value those engagements sufficiently to stick to the rules. When children generate the rules themselves, perhaps with a little help and revision over time, they are more likely to value the rules. However, they are more likely to generate productive rules when they have experienced, and thought about, more and less productive conversations. The first thing to do, then, is to arrange for children to have engaging and productive conversations, and then help them think about what made the conversations engaging and productive so they can take control of repeating the experience.

There are some simple strategies and expectations we want children to learn. For example, when they contribute to a conversation by disagreeing, they are responsible for supplying the logic of their position. They have the same responsibility when they agree. Doing so at once makes thinking available for others and makes disagreements not about the person, which would invite performance goals, but about the ideas and the logic. In fact, we encourage children to notice when no logic is supplied and to ask for it, even showing them how: "Why do you think that?" or "Could you explain?" When necessary, we prompt children to say "I agree, because . . . ," or "I disagree, because . . ." We can teach them that they can also simply add information—"And . . ." or "I agree, and . . ." or "I have evidence"—or add a qualifier— "Sometimes . . ." What they can't do is make it personal, because that will invite performance goals. The conversation has to be about ideas, logic, evidence, and possibilities. When disagreement shifts from ideas to relational conflicts, there is no end of trouble. Apart from anything else, participants become less open to change, they become more strident in their position, and they offer less justification for it.[23]

We expect everyone to participate. If the group is looking for agreement on a decision, everyone has to participate, because the group and its members will be responsible for the decision and because we want the best decision possible. Besides, we don't want someone after the fact saying "It wasn't my idea." Disagreement in the process of reaching agreement can ensure a better decision or outcome. Each person's experience, what they notice, the logic they bring, and the assumptions they don't accept enrich the conversation and, if we are trying to solve a problem, makes a solution more likely. If we are discussing a book, or movie, or an idea, we might not be looking for agreement, but simply a rich dialogue. In that case, we also want children to follow a line of thinking, keeping it open and focused in order to explore its depths.

In each case, we expect everyone to participate because being heard is a primary indicator of respect. It is not only in our own interests to encourage others to speak up, it is our moral obligation. Nonetheless, once we are caught up in an interesting discussion, it is easy to forget. Maria Nichols quotes Monique, a fourth-grade student, reflecting on her group's talk behavior during reading:[24]

> *I tried not to be a dominator, and I asked Shaun and Dareanna what they were thinking because we hadn't heard their voices yet. Everybody respected all the ideas. Well, a few people didn't listen, but we talked about that, and Shaun—he had really good thinking, and it made us all talk a lot, and all of it made me change my mind . . . [but] we kinda had a problem because some kids still didn't talk. So we didn't hear all the good ideas, maybe. . . . Maybe because we still don't be sure to ask the shy people. We get busy talking and forget. They may think we don't care how they think.*

Monique captures everything we aspire to as children take their thinking together as an object of study. She shows how and why she values thinking together, both the self-serving aspects and, through her mind reading, the altruistic caring aspects of it—the moral obligation.

At some point, we will want children to articulate and post on the wall a version of these social rules, preferably an ongoing draft. In the meantime, though, we arrange for them to act appropriately and then help them to articulate what they have done and why it is important. After arranging for groups of people to have productive discussions, I have often asked them to write out the rules of their thinking together. There is remarkable similarity in their lists. Here is an example related to problem solving:

- Listen, and respect each other's ideas.
- Everyone gets to be heard.
- We give reasons when we agree or disagree, and we ask for reasons when people forget to give them.
- Everyone is responsible for group decisions, so we try to agree.

You will find the same with children who have had productive experiences. The idea is to arrange for them to have a productive experience and then capitalize on it by generating community rules so that the successful experience becomes their typical experience. Because children will generate the rules for their conversations, each classroom will be different, but because they are guided by the teacher, and their experiences will be similar, the rules will be comparable. The rules cannot be simply presented by the teacher. The children have to generate them from an understanding of the social and intellectual logic. The rules must be merely markers for a social logic the children already know and support, otherwise the rules will be enforced through an authoritarian relationship, which is not good preparation for democratic life.

As we have already discovered, we want all children to participate in sharing their ideas, which means speaking up and listening actively and asking questions as necessary. We want them to be engaged in building ideas or solutions by using each other's thinking and linking ideas. We want children to realize that although they are trying to reach a shared conclusion, challenges and disagreements are expected, even encouraged, because they are useful for uncovering assumptions and new possibilities, and for making reasoning public. We want children to realize that when the group thinking is working well, it is more powerful and more engaging than their individual thinking, because it is.[25]

Probably the greatest source of innovation in the United States has been the diversity of its population, though innovation is commonly misattributed to less significant factors, and we have just as often viewed diversity as a handicap. As a highly individualistic society, we often attribute successes to individual greatness and tend not to notice the team of people on whose shoulders the success rests. Events happen, but we attach our own explanatory narrative. This is why having the experience of thinking together productively is important, but not enough. We still have to help children make sense of the experience. We can have the rule that everybody gets to participate because it is the teacher's requirement (as the authority), or because it is fair, or because it benefits everyone. Each of these can be compelling arguments. The second two are more compelling than the first, but in the long run the third, because it benefits everybody, is the most valuable because it is self-serving as well as other-serving. When a practice is narrated with this logic, it is more likely to occur even when the teacher is not present. This is why we add causal process observations like "I notice, Laurel, that when he was talking it sort of jogged your mind   what were you thinking?"[26] When our students turn and talk or begin to work as a group of three or four, we might say, "Make sure each person has a chance to say something so that you're sure you don't miss different ways of thinking about it." To encourage genuine disagreement, we might say, "Thanks Damon and Zelda. If you hadn't disagreed, we never would have got to the bottom of that." We want children to value the conversations and, as with any language genre, to have a sense of how conversations work and what they accomplish.

Revising the Process of Working Together

Having children develop rules to guide their classroom behavior is important, but it doesn't reduce the need for routine reflection on and debugging of group processes. After group activities, reviewing the way things went is no different from reviewing the process of solving a math problem or completing a science experiment. In the review process, we develop a metalanguage for thinking about group processes and establish their significance as something to attend to—something we have agency in.

In Susie Althof's kindergarten classroom the children are used to these debriefings and are able to initiate them themselves when they feel the need for problem solving. For example, on one occasion, after reading time at the end of the day, when they might have had a class meeting anyway, Mario asked Susie for one:

Susie: I've had a request for a class meeting, so let's go to class meeting. Mario has something that he'd like to talk about. . . . Let's get started. Eyes should be on your friend Mario because he called the meeting. Something's on his mind.

Mario: The people who was working with Ms. Althof with the books of frogs it was a little bit noisy then I cannot hear Osahar. I ask that next time people need to be a little bit quieter.
(There are lots of "sorry," "we're very sorry," etc., from class members.)

Susie: Well now, let's think about that. So you're saying that the people at my table *(the guided reading group)* were a little bit noisy. So we were giving you guys a hard time hearing? Huh. So what does everybody need to think about? If the people at my table are noisy it bothers . . .

Students: Us/all the people *(etc.)*

Susie: And if you guys at centers are noisy it bothers the . . .

Students: People at your table.

Susie: So what should we do about that?

Students: Fix it!

Susie: But how? We need some ideas. We can't just say be quiet
because we need to actually . . .

Student: Do it!

Susie: So how could we actually help each other do it?
*(Denzel leans over and models whispering to his neighbor, and
Susie points to this.)*

Susie: Would we just yell across the room, "Hey, you guys are
too loud"?

Students: No!

Susie: What would you do? *(Various ideas are offered.)* Look what
Denzel's doing. He's *showing* you right now. And if somebody
comes up to you and asks you like that—politely—to quiet
down would you say, "Oh, leave me alone"?

Students: No.

Susie: What would you say if someone asks you to quiet down?
(Lots of ideas.) . . . So if somebody walks up to my table while
we're working and says "You guys are a little bit noisy," what
should we do? *(Students respond with quiet down, etc.)* We
should be quiet and say thank you for reminding us and we'll
try to calm down. And you know, some people really need it
to be quiet for them to think and write. How many of you
feel you don't mind the noise? *(Susie puts up her hand.)* How
many of you prefer it when it's calm and quiet? *(Most raise
their hands.).* Oooh. Look how many of us prefer calm and
quiet. Is that something we need to work on?

Students: Yes.

This is such a rich conversation that I have unpacked its detail in
Appendix B. You probably noticed how Susie made sure children
understood that the noise problem wasn't her problem, but our
problem because of its consequences for others. She frames the situation as one of positive interdependence; that is, the children's goals,
relationships, and community life are bound together. When children understand that their own performance has consequences for
their group mates, it increases their sense of responsibility and
involvement in the class's efforts, which increases their efforts to
achieve.[27] Cooperative classrooms like this foster more positive relationships, including across ethnic groups and between handicapped

and nonhandicapped students, and these generalize beyond academic settings to free-choice interactions.[28] Because of this, and because Susie has fostered positive relationships among the children, they feel even more responsibility,[29] which is why, she points out, when we forget and someone politely helps us to be responsible, we should be appreciative.

Susie made it clear that solving the group's problem (no longer just Mario's) is normal and requires practical strategies, which she asks the children to generate, and particular ways of talking, which she demonstrates. At the same time, she finds the opportunity to remind the children that everyone is different—some prefer quiet, others not so much—and asks them to view things from others' perspectives. This social interdependence that Susie is building has important consequences. A meta-analysis of over 1,200 studies comparing cooperative structures that foster social interdependence with competitive and individualistic structures showed strong effects on achievement, interpersonal attraction, social support, self-esteem, time on task, attitudes toward task, quality of reasoning, and perspective taking.[30] The size of the effects ranged between nearly a half to over a full standard deviation. When students experience low-maintenance relationships, they actually have better self-regulation than when they experience high-maintenance relationships.[31] Indeed, we tend to think about self-regulation as an individual phenomenon, but social systems also self-regulate and it is through individuals' active co-participation in those self-regulating social systems that self-regulation develops at the individual level. In fact, self-regulation and other regulation are inextricably linked in self-regulating social systems.[32]

The effectiveness of cooperative structures that foster social interdependence is one of the most thoroughly researched areas in educational psychology, and at some point we will have to start taking it seriously. Perhaps we need to assess it, as they have in the National Educational Monitoring Project (NEMP), New Zealand's equivalent of the National Assessment of Educational Progress (NAEP) in the United States. The NEMP is not a high-stakes test, because such a test would jeopardize the conditions that make productive thinking together possible.[33] In the NEMP, they use test items like the following: Give a group of four fourth-grade students a set of books. Their job is to act as the library committee and individually, then collectively, decide which books the committee should buy. The process is videotaped and scored against a rubric. Changes in the ability to engage in collaborative activities are documented as a matter of national interest. It is, after all, a democracy, and this sort of ability is fundamental to democratic living. Indeed, we can think of democracy as a good form of government or we can think of it as a way of living together within which we become better, more developed people— individually and collecively.

CHAPTER 9

Choice Worlds

The life and work of the school should contribute, in every possible way, to the physical, mental and emotional health of every student.
—Wilford Aikin[1]

Teaching must be advocacy: for kids, for democracy, for a better world. If it is not advocacy for those ideals, then it is advocacy for something else.
—Randy and Katherine Bomer[2]

It is December, and Susie Althof asks her kindergartners, "Do we have a job when we're in Webster [Elementary School]?" Her students respond, in this order:

"To learn."
"To be friendly."
"To care and be friends."
"To laugh."

There is more than a pinch of sanity in this class. The children like being in school. In fact, when Susie explains later in the year that when Eric Carle was a young boy he didn't like to go to school, their faces register shock. Are they academically successful? I can't think of a kindergarten class in which children are learning more academically.

Learning is, after all, the first item on their agenda. Is that the limit of what they are gaining? Not by a long way. These children are becoming fully equipped for socially, emotionally, morally, and intellectually complex and engaged lives. They care for each other and take pleasure (mostly—and increasingly) in that caring. They are learning to manage their relationships with each other through thick and thin and to value equity and diversity inside and outside the classroom.

Susie wants her kindergarten students to have meaningful lives and she wants them to know how to construct them. She wants them to become teachers—whether or not they take up that occupation later in life. When Qadir asks for Susie's help to spell *spaghetti*, Susie assesses the situation and sees that Adrianna, who is sitting next to him, has done a pretty fair job of writing *hamburger*. So Susie turns to Adrianna and explains what she has done successfully and adds, "I have an idea for you. You did such a good job writing *hamburger*, stretching your sounds, I think you could help him with *spaghetti*. How could you help him?" Adrianna responds that they could stretch the sounds. "Stretch the sounds?" Susie has Adrianna practice showing how to sound out an easy word, *man*, while Qadir is watching and then leaves so the teaching can be done. Coming back presently she says, "Look at that. He's writing it down. Aren't you happy for your partner?" Then catching her later by herself, Susie says to Adrianna, "Did you help your partner?" This draws a big smile and a nod. "How does that feel?" she asks, helping Adrianna recognize the pleasure—the happiness—in meaningful social action.[3]

In the fourth grade, Jeralyn Johnson takes the same stance, teaching students to be teachers as well as learners. Observing a group working together, she points out how one student supported another student. "You know what? You didn't just give him the answer and that's important because giving him the answer doesn't make him think any harder—I see you wanted to, but you stopped yourself." These interactions are about teaching teachers. They are also about communities and cultures—oh, and classroom management too. It turns out that when children feel a sense of competence and relational significance—that they contribute to the community—they are more likely to respect its norms and have a sense of place. They understand that their interests are linked to the interests of the community—an important part of democratic living. Imagine the implications of twelve (or even eight) years of this instruction as these children become parents and teachers.

Teaching for Economic Survival

Efforts at educational reform have not taken seriously the significance of what children in classrooms like Susie Althof's and Jeralyn Johnson's are learning—for children's development, for the society for which the children will ultimately take responsibility, and for children's academic success. We have focused on the nation's and individual children's presumed economic survival. According to the White House website, the "Guiding Principles" for our nation's reinvestment in education are that "providing a high-quality education for all children is critical to America's economic future. Our nation's economic competitiveness and the path to the American Dream depend on providing every child with an education that will enable them to succeed in a global economy."[4] We have only taken seriously children's academic success and that only in the narrowest terms and largely for its economic benefit—also with the narrowest vision. The primary tool for reform has been increased pressure toward performance goals: teach more to get better test scores or be punished.

This single-minded and highly controlling view has blinded us to the fact that when children grow up, they are not only going to be wage earners. They are going to be citizens, parents, spouses, teachers, politicians, artists, managers, and so forth. Do we want them to become successful in these endeavors—citizens who actively work toward a just democracy, effective parents and spouses, lifelong learners, effective teachers, creative and collaborative workmates? I think we do. Should we assume that these goals will take care of themselves if we just attend to academics? The evidence suggests otherwise. Would working toward those goals hinder the development of wage earning ability? The evidence says the reverse. Do these accomplishments themselves have economic impact?

Consider what happens when children's development goes awry and they turn to crime. The United States has a higher percentage of the population incarcerated than any other country, at considerable cost to society, communities, and individuals. We have the largest prison population in the world, with 4 percent of the world's population and 25 percent of the world's incarcerated population. The U.S. Department of Justice estimates that the 23 million recorded criminal offences in 2007 cost the immediate victims $15 billion and the government $179 billion for law enforcement, legal, and corrections activities, and that's just the economic cost, not the pain and suffering,

psychological distress, and diminished quality of life.[5] Similarly, consider what happens when we don't attend to the whole development of
the child. In the United States, untreated (and *unprevented*) mental
health problems such as mood and anxiety disorders and depression
cost the society close to $200 billion per year in lost earnings alone.
The cost of addiction disorders is estimated at $500 billion. That isn't
counting the personal and relational costs or the cost of treatment
when it actually occurs.[6]

If the "American dream" has a lot to do with "the pursuit of happiness," neglecting broader aspects of children's development will not
help. Failure to attend to children's moral and social development will
lead neither to happiness nor to economic security. Happiness matters
even if you focus on economics. Happy teenagers ultimately have much
higher incomes than those who are less happy, even after accounting for
family income and grades.[7] But happiness, it turns out, is made up of
three parts: "the pleasant life" (pleasure), "the engaged life," and "the
meaningful life," and pursuit of the latter two, meaning and engagement, are the best predictors of life satisfaction.[8]

Our main advantage as human beings lies in our ability to think
together. Our main threat has become our failure to think and act
together on larger scales and to act on the understanding that the sheer
existence of our species depends on how we think together—how we
experience and treat each other. We can think of this as an autoimmune
disorder. In recent years in the United States the number of people
experiencing physiological autoimmune disorders has grown quite rapidly, and there is reason to believe that this growth is associated with
increasing stress.[9] Prolonged stress can confuse the immune system's
ability to distinguish between foreign invaders and parts of the body, so
the immune system ends up attacking the body. Stress in learning communities produces a similar response. As we saw in Chapter 5, under
stress, we often take up fixed theories about people and ideas. We
stereotype and begin to view difference as a threat. We shut down any
ideas unlike our own and turn against the source of those ideas.
Without difference, creativity drops, and the community's ability to
deal with novel threats becomes restricted. As the emotional and relational fabric of the community is undermined, the ability of the community to learn, adapt, nurture, and grow further deteriorates.

In other words, framing education as centrally about economic
competitiveness and the improvement of education as about increasing
pressure on individuals to perform better is not a promising strategy.
We need a better vision to guide education. The vision of humanity that

we help children construct within our classroom practice changes who they think they are, how they view each other, and thus how they treat each other. Conceptualizing successful schooling in terms of our vision of humanity should make us imbue test scores with less authority than we currently do.

The Moment and the Future

We might choose to focus on teaching the two subjects that the students are commonly tested in but, whether we like to think about it or not, we are teaching the whole child and the associated vision of society. Before we forget, then, let me just repeat that the children in Susie Althof's class like being at school. They are generally happy at school because they are living meaningful and engaged lives. Happier people are more successful, more socially engaged, and healthier, and the causal arrows point in both directions.[10] In our big plans for reform, the significance of this aspect of schooling is often lost. Once I was on a state curriculum committee making big plans for children's language arts instruction when I learned that my five-year-old niece, Gloria, had been diagnosed with leukemia with a one in four chance of survival. What would be the best curriculum for Gloria, I wondered? Now that she is in her twenties, would I change my mind? I don't think so. We can't teach for the future without attending to the moments of today. Each day counts and each is made up of moments.

Not only does each day count, but they add up to something. Over time, we become disposed to act in particular ways. When Jeralyn Johnson says to her fourth-grade students, "I want to share not just the details, but the process of what you went through," she is keeping their experience as much as possible within a dynamic learning frame. This frame is reinforced everywhere. A class motto is "It's OK for things to be hard. That's when we learn. We show we believe in ourselves by saying things like 'I don't get it yet.'" The students regularly make compatible observations that Jeralyn capitalizes on. A signed and dated quote on the wall from one of her students is "It's not about being the best, it's about trying your best."[11] Each is an instance of a strong and persistent current in the talk of her classroom. By themselves these statements are each important for reminding students which world we are living in. Repeated over and over in their many different forms, they shape children's consciousness. Children begin to be disposed to act in particular ways. As we learned in Chapters 2, 3, and 4, a history of this kind of interaction and associated experiences promotes a disposition toward resilience, "the tendency to maintain a focus on learning when the going gets tough. It's opposite is brittleness—the tendency to avoid challenging tasks and to shift into ego-defensive behaviors when learning is difficult."[12]

Setting children up to have experiences that dispose them toward reciprocity is equally important: "Oh, Quay, you just did something important. You said 'Your turn' to your partner" and "Say something to your partner about how they helped you today." The disposition toward reciprocity is "a willingness to engage in joint learning tasks, to express uncertainties and ask questions, to take a variety of roles in joint learning enterprises and to take others' purposes and perspectives into account."[13] Much of the book has addressed the development of this disposition.

Because of its link to the golden rule, reciprocity holds within it the seeds of another disposition—a disposition toward social justice. We want our children to recognize when things are unfair and to act to make things right. We saw this in Mary Cowhey's class when second grader Thomas and his colleagues wrote a letter to the U.S. Treasury requesting that they remove images of slave owners from our country's coins and replace them with images of people who lived more just lives. This comes from classrooms where it is normal for children to confront, think through, and act on moral dilemmas, particularly using their social imaginations to explore the issues from multiple perspectives. If someone is being bullied, we want them to recognize the bullying and act in a way that will help restore equity. This is not a hypothetical problem. Half of American students say they have been bullied in the past year—and half say they have bullied.[14]

The cultures we establish in classrooms also influence the kinds of justice children will be disposed toward. Do we want them to be disposed toward retributive justice—an eye for an eye—as fixed-frame thinkers emphasize? A judgmental classroom will get us there, even if most of the judgments are positive. Or do we want them to be disposed toward restorative justice, where the perpetrator must act to restore balance to the victim and his or her community? Educative approaches such as this are more valued in a dynamic frame. These experiences are also conveyed in the ways we act and explain our actions in dealing with classroom transgressions. As Ruth Charney points out, dealing with transgressions requires the following:

- A concrete, here-and-now focus. The teacher does not give opinions, make judgments, or offer interpretations.

- A straightforward and matter-of-fact tone. The teacher tries to name the 'deeds' openly and accurately, without blame or severity.
- Fact-finding as a method of thinking. The teacher models an approach that requires information gathering before conclusions are drawn and solutions are considered.[15]

These principles are the foundations for ways of being together, ways of thinking about and acting toward self and other, and they reflect fundamental beliefs about humanity. They are ways of thinking that are not separate from academic learning.

Relatively few studies of teaching take a broad, long-term view of children's learning and development in school. Such studies do exist though. In the 1930s a large group of American high schools changed their instructional practices over a period of time toward an inquiry curriculum, and over eight years tracked the implications for students' learning using a wide array of tests. They found that their students did better on the academic standardized tests, but that wasn't all. Their intellectual, cultural, and emotional development also improved, as did their sensitivity to social problems and their social and moral competence. Their interests also expanded.[16]

Just Teaching

I have often heard teachers during social introductions refer to their work as "just teaching." Many in the public, the media, and in politics take this dismissive view. In this book, I hope I have shown that teachers' work should not be underestimated. The only way teachers should refer to "just teaching" is when referring to the kind of teaching in which they are engaged—teaching for justice. There are several ways to think about what that might mean. The most common concern regarding justice and teaching is equality of opportunity. This is certainly an important focus; however, this is commonly translated into ensuring that all children achieve sufficiently well on tests to go to college and successfully compete with everyone else for well-paying jobs.[17] This view of fairness is that education will put everyone on the same starting line in the race to the top, thus making it possible to justify as fair the failure of many others to get the well-paying jobs.[18] But children start from different places and take different paths. I cannot conceive of the possibility of all children achieving equally in everything nor accept that arranging for that to happen would be fair to everyone, or productive.

A better concept of a fair education would be to try to have every child develop as fully as possible. Of course we have no way of knowing what is possible for each child. All we can do is arrange for children to be fully engaged in ways that we know lead to expanded development. Striving for full engagement seems like an excellent goal, and one that has been neglected in the rush to standardize outcomes. When children are fully engaged in an activity, they press into service all of their resources and stretch themselves as necessary. Children are more engaged when they have choice, a degree of autonomy, and when they see the activity as relevant. Full engagement might not guarantee equal outcomes, but it will equalize the likelihood that children capitalize on learning opportunities.

Let me give you a sense of how this might work. In one middle school, the four eighth-grade English teachers collectively decided to stop assigning texts for the students to read.[19] Instead, they introduced the students to edgy young adult fiction, which the students could choose to read. Choice, along with the fact that the narratives were relevant to their lives, hooked most students fairly quickly. The average number of books read per year went from three to forty-two. The fact that the books were edgy and morally (and textually) complex meant not only that the eighth graders couldn't put the books down but also that they couldn't stop thinking about the books. This, along with the intensity of the reading experiences, compelled the students to solicit each other's perspectives in order to make more sense and expand the experience. This meant that some students applied strong relational pressure on others to participate in the reading and conversations in order to share the experience, drawing in most of the holdouts. The resulting spontaneous, sustained conversations inside and outside of school around the books focused on moral dilemmas and placed considerable demands on social imaginations. Teachers did less explicit teaching of strategies (not as much time, as the students were reading), yet students became more strategic in their drive to understand and participate. "Silent reading" gave way to as-needed conversations. Because of their deep engagement, this did not interrupt those who were still reading.

Quinton, a student in special education with a limited history of reading and no prior history of passing a state test, made this observation:[20]

I read books about peoples' lives. Homeboyz *[Sitomer 2007].* Rucker Park Setup *[Volponi 2007].* War of the Blood in My

Veins [Morris 2008]. They're in gangs and they seek redemption.
That word comes up a lot in the book I'm reading now . . . My mom
was shocked when I asked her for books. She said, "Quinton, I don't
know if you've matured or what." I've told her it's a new lifestyle. It
makes me think about things that I do before I do them. I used to do
things before thinking. Now I think about the consequences.

The moral agency reflected in Quinton's final comments should be taken no less seriously than his passing the state competency test for the first time.

Discussing the books opened more possibilities not only for expanding social imagination and for contemplating moral logic, but for transforming social relationships. For example, when a group of students discussed *A Long Way Gone: Memoirs of a Boy Soldier*[21] Frank pointed out that the author, growing up in Sierra Leone, lived with no water or electricity. This prompted a confession from Tommy that transformed the relationships in the group and enabled Tommy to offer an important narrative:[22]

Simon: How can someone in this day and time still not have water and power in their house?

Tommy: We don't have water, me and my mom.
(*silence*)

Ginny: You have water.

Tommy: We have water, but when me and my mom need it I go to the well down from the house and bring some in.

Frank: The guy in the book had to get it from a river.
(*everyone is looking at Tommy*)

Ginny: How do you do the laundry?

Marco: Or take a bath?

Tommy: We have to make a lot of trips to the well. We can't waste any water.

Simon: Did the guy in the book become a soldier because he could get like water and a better life?

Frank: No, it was other stuff.

Tommy: Not having running water wouldn't make you do bad things, I don't think.

Ben: No, he had a good family. They told old family stories, and they got killed by some soldiers and that's why he got left alone.

Ginny: I want to know how the well works. It's probably good you know how to get your own water. I wouldn't know what to do if my faucet stopped working.

Tommy: Me and my mom know how to do a lot of things around the house.

In another context, this expanded understanding of a peer and of different ways of living might not have occurred. Worse, it might have occurred without Tommy's consent, and been cause for others to torment him. It certainly might not have been cast as the agentive narrative Tommy is able to offer.

There are important transformations taking place in these conversations. At the community level, we can hear in this transcript a developing level of trust. Indeed, when students have the opportunity for dialogic interaction, there is an increase in social trust without which it becomes very difficult to run a democracy, but which has been systematically declining.[23] There are also personal transformations. These eighth graders are collaboratively thinking through moral dilemmas in slow motion and in detail before they actually encounter them in real life (in most cases). Along with development of their social imagination, this leads students to act in new ways, as one student observed:

Yeah, like I read a couple of books where people get bullied, and it changes my mind, cause in a couple of books I read people commit suicide for it. And . . . Hate List, that book is really good and it changes my mind about how people feel about things. And even like a little comment can change someone's life. And like the other day I saw people on Facebook picking on this one girl, like saying nobody liked her because she was ugly and had no friends. And I kind of put a stop to it. I told them it was wrong and that people commit suicide for it all the time. So it changed my way of seeing things. Normally I wouldn't have said anything to stop. But now, if I see anything, I stop it.[24]

That these students are thinking through social problems in their school lives—bullying, discrimination, loneliness—using the books as vehicles, expanding their social imaginations and their relational ties, should be celebrated more than their test scores. The fact that about 15 percent more of these children now pass the state competency test might be more persuasive to some, but it is perhaps worth noting that this is in spite of, or perhaps because of, the fact that the teachers are spending less time overtly "teaching" the students to read and more time listening. They are offering the students the opportunity to work on making sense of their lives and to build a sense of autonomy. Reading and the resulting conversations have simply become a tool for doing so. The teachers' brief instruction during read-aloud has become a tool for some of the students in their quests, but much of the instruction comes from other students in more symmetrical power contexts.

Learning opportunities are more equalized, or at least democratized, when children know how to think together and when they are collaboratively working to solve or create something. Optimal learning is more likely, too, if children can avoid fixed-frame worlds. In these eighth-grade classrooms, the engagements are dialogic, and there are no obvious ways or reasons to compare children with one another or otherwise invoke performance goals or a fixed frame. Such practices can lead to optimizing each child's academic development and certainly go some way to reducing achievement differences. However, optimal academic learning, while important, would still be a very limited vision of a just education. Academic learning alone doesn't prepare children to continue the work of building a society "with liberty and justice for all"—the vision to which we aspire. And there surely is work yet to be done in this construction.

Working toward this vision requires recognizing that schools, and particularly classrooms, are places where the principles that hold our society and its citizens together are negotiated and embodied, whether consciously or not. It requires that our classrooms become places in which the complexities of justice in its daily and worldly forms are normal topics of conversation and action so that children value justice and develop a sufficiently complex moral vocabulary for naming and negotiating it. I hope I have shown in this book that these goals are not incompatible with academic goals. Indeed, they are synergistic. The values of just teaching are embedded in our actions and in the logic through which we justify our actions.[25] Do we study science because that's where the money is or because it can help make a better world? Do we not steal because there is a rule and punishment, or because of its consequences for others?

Doing Meaningful Things

Most statements of "standards" or educational goals include the concept of children becoming "lifelong learners." Yet in general we fail to arrange for children to play any active role in deciding the purposes of their learning. Indeed, for many children, very little of what they do in school is personally meaningful. With some exceptions,[26] we do not have children actually trying to accomplish things in the world—trying to make change. This deprives them of the feeling of generosity, agency, and courageousness, along with the bonding that occurs when people work together to accomplish something. We have to teach toward children who, individually and collaboratively, make meaning and do meaningful things.

The following transcript from Maria Nichols's book *Comprehension Through Conversation* shows Jesse Harrison's third graders complete a third reading conversation around Cynthia Rylant's book *An Angel for Solomon Singer* and come to grips with how the character is feeling and why. Notice that five children are contributing and the teacher's role is relatively small in terms of number of words.[27]

Kiarra: Sometimes when people leave their home, sometimes they, um, miss their home and wish for what they're used to. He's (*Solomon Singer*) used to Indiana. But now he doesn't really have a home, and that's sad.

Keysha: When you're at home, you have friends, and you have confidence. Everything's what you're used to.

Ramika: But at the men's hotel, there's probably no one there that likes him, nobody in there that takes care of him. That's why he's going to the West Way Café.

Edward: Now, he has friends and confidence. People need it to feel at home.

Dianna: Yeah, that's true because I was scared here at first when I was new here, but now it feels like home.

Jesse: So, this is something that happens in the real world. Do you think that's what this story is really about?

Keysha: It's about how we can make people feel at home, like Angel did. He's like a lesson for us. But I think it's what we should do.

Jesse: Can we take this on right here at Webster?

Kiarra: Whenever we know someone's new or doesn't feel at home, we can welcome them.

The students link this to their own experiences because of the kind of conversation they have become used to. They are using their social imaginations to understand the characters. They are using the characters to understand themselves. They are reading for meaning. But Jesse moves them two more steps. First, Dianna makes a personal connection to being scared and alone in a new place and the transformation to feeling at home. Jesse raises this up, saying, "So, this is something that happens in the real world," helping them to take the meaning they made in the book and move it out into their world.

Up to this point, they have been taking their world into the book. Now they take that world from the book back to make sense of their world, as Keysha adds, "It's what we should do."

But it's still not enough for Jesse. She asks, "Can we take this on right here at Webster?" She invites them to make the abstract concrete—not in the book, but in their immediate lives.

Kiarra picks up the imaginative request and says, "Whenever we know someone's new or doesn't feel at home, we can welcome them."

Jesse's question is the lever that makes the shift from "reading for meaning" to "reading for meaningful action." As Maria points out, the students are "beginning to envision acting on their understanding to create a more just world."[28] It starts with those two utterances of Jesse's—and of course, others like them during readings of other books. In effect, Jesse says to her students, "Now you know, what are you going to do about it?"

In the end, if we are to take seriously "research-based" teaching, we should remember that the research shows us these things:

1. Our singular focus on individual academic achievement will not serve children or their academic development well, either in the short term or the long term. Intelligence, creativity, and caring are all properties of communities as much as of individuals, and teaching children with that in mind will result in individual achievement but also collaborative achievement and accompanying social and societal benefits.

2. The individual achievement view that everyone should know the same things in the same way and be individually excellent in all areas means that collectively we are no more intelligent than we are individually. The individual mind is important, no doubt, but as the center of the academic universe, it is overrated.

3. We have to take seriously the fact that the adult is not the only teacher in the room.

4. Children's social imaginations should be taken more seriously. They are the foundation of civic society, but they are also central to children's ability to think together (and thus the development of their thinking alone) and to their moral and social development.

5. Our interactions with children in the classroom influence who they think they are and what they think they're doing. Over time, the interactions affect children's values and dispositions—how they value learning, themselves and each other, and whether they become disposed toward resilience, reciprocity, and social justice.

6. Making meaning is good. Doing meaningful things is better.

Ultimately, we have to generate a more productive vision for society than the one that has been guiding schooling, and we must equip children with what they need to construct that society. Given what we know, failing to attend to students' civic, social, and broader cognitive development in school is not only academically short-changing children, it is criminal.

Well, now you know . . .

Jackie Robinson Conversation

Joshua:	He said he'll need guts—that's saying courage—because white people won't like that he's getting to play.	
Cheryl:	So why do you think Jackie agreed? What does this tell us about him . . . ?	The "why do you think . . ." is an open invitation to make thinking public. The question takes Joshua's response seriously, recognizing his authority and establishing respect. The history of nonjudgment in these discussions allows "What does this tell us about him?" to not be viewed as a monologic question. It might be better phrased as, "Does this suggest anything to you about Jackie?"
Joshua:	He said yes so he can play.	
Jonathan:	No, no, I think . . .	
Cheryl:	Ah, Jonathan, it sounds like you have a different idea?	Recognizes Jonathan's authority, . . .
Jonathan:	(Shakes head yes.)	
Cheryl:	Will you hold on to it until we dig into Joshua's idea? Let's hear his evidence before we move on to a new idea. Joshua, what makes you think that's the reason?	. . . but guides the students to develop the idea that is already on the table—to allow Joshua, who now knows there are different views, to clarify and offer evidence for his thinking. The questions to both Jonathan and Joshua assume that they are engaged, thinking people. The question to Joshua reminds the students of the need to provide evidence to support their ideas.
Joshua:	Because he was the star in college—but he couldn't be on a team because of racism.	
Cheryl:	What do the rest of you think?	Taking herself out of the authoritative, judging position, she asks the group to take Joshua's thinking seriously, positioning them as knowledgeable, thinking people.

Kayla:	It said that was how the world was back then. So he had to say yes, because he could get a chance (*to play*). He couldn't get a chance before. They didn't care he was the star because he was black.	Kayla elaborates a logic to support Joshua's thinking.
Jonathan:	But Kayla, he . . . well, he . . . yeah, he probably did want to play, but it's like Martin Luther King Jr. He always said don't fight. And the book said . . .	Jonathan sets out to disagree, recognizes that he partly agrees, but offers an alternative perspective, making links to other examples and to the book. In the process, he positions Kayla and Joshua as thinking people, but offers a different source of logic and evidence.
Theresea:	Oh! It's like *The Other Side* (*referring to the book by Jacqueline Woodson, which the students had read, thought, and talked about together*)! It said about the wall—on the other page (*referring to the "Then and Now" section*). It's like the fence. He (*Jackie Robinson*) knows it shouldn't be.	Theresea takes up Jonathan's view, makes a new metaphorical link, and infers the thinking of Jackie Robinson.
Marta:	Oh, yeah. I didn't think about that!	Marta recognizes that her classmate has given her a new idea, a new perspective.
Cheryl:	So you're constructing a new theory for why Jackie agreed not to fight back. What does everyone think about this idea (*looking questioningly around the circle*)?	Cheryl articulates what the students are doing, constructing theories. She does not rearticulate the theory, which would reduce the need for the students to listen to each other, but invites further engagements and makes it clear she wants to hear what they have to say.
Ben:	No, I don't get it—what Theresea said.	Ben admits to the teacher that he does not understand his classmate.
Cheryl:	When you don't understand what someone said, remember, it's your job to ask them to explain.	Cheryl points out who should receive that comment, in the process leveling the power structure, taking herself out of the authority position and explaining that in a dialogic classroom there are responsibilities.
Ben:	(*looking at Theresea*) I don't get what you mean.	

From Nichols (2008). Some author annotations specific to Nichols's text have been edited out of the transcript to avoid confusion.

Mario's Class Meeting

Susie:	I've had a request for a class meeting, so let's go to class meeting. Mario has something that he'd like to talk about. . . . Let's get started. Eyes should be on your friend Mario because he called the meeting. Something's on his mind.	Susie makes it clear that students, such as Mario, have authority and things to say. She removes herself from the center of authority.
Mario:	The people who was working with Ms. Althof with the books of frogs it was a little bit noisy then I cannot hear Osahar. I ask that next time people need to be a little bit quieter.	By critiquing his teacher's group, Mario shows that Susie has been successful at removing herself from the center of authority. Mario presents his concern with its social logic.
Students:	Sorry Sorry We're very sorry	Students are genuinely apologetic, recognizing the consequences of their behavior for a peer.
Susie:	Well now, let's think about that. So you're saying that the people at my table (*the guided reading group*) were a little bit noisy. So we were giving you guys a hard time hearing? Huh. So what does everybody need to think about? If the people at my table are noisy it bothers . . .	Susie reiterates the causal sequence of the problem and invites solutions.
Students:	Us/all the people (*etc.*)	
Susie:	And if you guys at centers are noisy it bothers the . . .	
Students:	People at your table.	
Susie:	So what should we do about that?	Susie repeats the invitation. By not asserting a solution, she leaves the students in control of social problem solving.
Students:	Fix it!	
Susie:	But how? We need some ideas. We can't just say be quiet because we need to actually . . .	Susie draws attention to *how*, focusing on specific strategies rather than general platitudes.

Student:	Do it!	
Susie:	So how could we actually help each other do it?	Susie doesn't remove the need for thinking about solutions by proposing one herself or by drawing attention to rules.
	(*Denzel leans over and models whispering to his neighbor and Susie points to this.*)	
Susie:	Would we just yell across the room, "Hey you guys are too loud"?	Susie offers a counter-example.
Students:	No!	
Susie:	What would you do? (*Various ideas are offered.*) Look what Denzel's doing. He's showing you right now. And if somebody comes up to you and asks you like that—politely—to quiet down would you say, "Oh leave me alone"?	Susie capitalizes on Denzel's demonstration, making him the teacher. She then poses a hypothetical social context to rehearse how to interact as peers supporting each other's behavior.
Students:	No.	
Susie:	What would you say if someone asks you to quiet down? (*Lots of ideas.*) . . . So if somebody walks up to my table while we're working and says "You guys are a little bit noisy," what should we do? (*Students respond with quiet down, etc.*) We should be quiet and say thank you for reminding us and we'll try to calm down. And you know, some people really need it to be quiet for them to think and write. How many of you feel you don't mind the noise? (*Susie puts up her hand.*) How many of you prefer it when it's calm and quiet? (*Most raise their hands.*). Oooh. Look how many of us prefer calm and quiet. Is that something we need to work on?	Susie frames peers providing feedback on behavior as a positive event—others helping us manage our behavior. Shows the psychological consequence of noisy behavior for others—extending the children's social imaginations and their recognition of the context for using social imagination. Susie shows the diversity of preference and makes it clear that working for a quieter classroom is not for her as the authority, but for the community because of peers' needs.
Students:	Yes.	

Notes

CHAPTER 1: CHOOSING WORDS, CHOOSING WORLDS

1. This transcript is from Maria Nichols's excellent book, *Comprehension Through Conversation: The Power of Purposeful Talk in the Reading Workshop*, 91.
2. Cazden, "Reflections on the Study of Classroom Talk," 163.

CHAPTER 2: LEARNING WORLDS: PEOPLE, PERFORMING, AND LEARNING

1. Halliday, "Towards a Language-Based Theory of Learning," 107.
2. From Ray, with Cleaveland, *About the Authors: Writing Workshop with Our Youngest Writers*, 102.
3. Tovani, *I Read It, but I Don't Get It*, 7.
4. Laczynski, "The Children Left Behind: Memories of Promoting Literacy," 403.
5. In my earlier book *Choice Words*, a student, when asked whether there are different kinds of readers in his class, said, "There's like the ones who's not good and the ones who are good."
6. Carol Dweck, in *Mindset: The New Psychology of Success*, calls this frame a "growth theory" since it allows for growth rather than remain fixed. I am calling it a dynamic theory because, later, I will apply a parallel idea to conceptions of knowledge, and that idea will include not only the idea of growth but also the idea that knowledge is context dependent. Dynamic captures the idea of change in both contexts.
7. Dweck, *Self-Theories: Their Role in Motivation, Personality, and Development*, 42.
8. Grant and Dweck, "Clarifying Achievement Goals and Their Impact," 541–553; Blackwell, Trzesniewski, and Dweck, "Implicit Theories of Intelligence Predict Achievement Across an Adolescent Transition: A Longitudinal Study and an Intervention," 246–263; Cury et al., "The Social-Cognitive Model of Achievement Motivation and the 2 × 2 Achievement Goal Framework," 666–679; Dweck and Leggett, "A Social-Cognitive Approach to Motivation and Personality, 256–273.
9. Dweck, *Self-Theories: Their Role in Motivation, Personality, and Development*, 42.
10. Nussbaum and Dweck, "Defensiveness vs. Remediation: Self-Theories and Modes of Self-Esteem Maintenance," 599–612.
11. McCloskey, "Taking on a Learning Disability: Negotiating Special Education and Learning to Read," 92.
12. Hong et al., "Implicit Theories, Attributions, and Coping: A Meaning System Approach," 588–599.
13. Ibid.

14. Diener and Dweck, "An Analysis of Learned Helplessness: Continuous Changes in Performance, Strategy, and Achievement Cognitions Following Failure," 451–462.
15. Diener and Dweck, "An Analysis of Learned Helplessness: II. The Processing of Success," 940–952.
16. Baird et al., "Cognitive Self-Regulation in Youth with and Without Learning Disabilities: Academic Self-Efficacy, Theories of Intelligence, Learning vs. Performance Goal Preferences, and Effort Attributions," 881–908.
17. Johnston and Champeau, "High Stakes Testing: Narratives of the Cost of 'Friendly Fire.'"
18. Blackwell, Trzesniewski, and Dweck, "Implicit Theories of Intelligence Predict Achievement Across an Adolescent Transition: A Longitudinal Study and an Intervention," 246–263.
19. Cimpian et al., "Subtle Linguistic Cues Affect Children's Motivation," 314–316.
20. Blackwell, Trzesniewski, and Dweck, "Implicit Theories of Intelligence Predict Achievement Across an Adolescent Transition: A Longitudinal Study and an Intervention," 246–263.
21. Johnston, Goatley, and Dozier, "Educator Decision-Making Orientation."
22. TeacherVision, "Character Traits."
23. Levy et al. "Static Versus Dynamic Theories and the Perception of Groups: Different Routes to Different Destinations," 156–168.
24. Plaks et al., "Person Theories and Attention Allocation: Preferences for Stereotypic Versus Counterstereotypic Information," 876–893.
25. Molden and Dweck, "Finding 'Meaning' in Psychology," 192–203.
26. Knee, "Implicit Theories of Relationships: Assessment and Prediction of Romantic Relationship Initiation, Coping and Longevity," 360–370.
27. Darnon et al., "Mastery and Performance Goals Predict Epistemic and Relational Conflict Regulation," 766–776.
28. Chiu et al., "Implicit Theories and Conceptions of Morality," 923–940; Erdley and Dweck, "Children's Implicit Personality Theories as Predictors of Their Social Judgments," 863–878; Heyman and Dweck, "Children's Thinking About Traits: Implications for Judgments of the Self and Others," 391–403.
29. Ibid.
30. Baer, Grant, and Dweck, "Personal Goals, Dysphoria, and Coping Strategies,"cited in Molden and Dweck, "Finding 'Meaning' in Psychology," 192–203.
31. Levy-Tossman, Kaplan, and Assor, "Academic Goal Orientations, Multiple Goal Profiles, and Friendship Intimacy Among Early Adolescents," 231–252.
32. The "zone of proximal development" is the space between what one can do independently and what one can't do even with collaborative support. The concept was developed by Lev Vygotsky, *Mind in Society*.

CHAPTER 3: CHANGING LEARNING NARRATIVES

1. Quoted in *The Week*, September 24, 2010, 21.
2. Located at http://plato.stanford.edu/entries/relativism/supplement1.html.
3. Indeed, Blackwell, Trzesniewski, and Dweck successfully used this strategy with middle school students, showing them that when you learn, your brain actually grows more neurons.
4. Delizonna, Williams, and Langer, "The Effect of Mindfulness on Heart Rate Control," 61–65.
5. Yanoff, "Inquiry and Ideological Becoming in First Grade Literature Discussions."
6. Ryan and Deci, "Self-Regulation and the Problem of Human Autonomy: Does Psychology Need Choice, Self-Determination, and Will?" 1557–1586.
7. Johnston, *Choice Words: How Our Language Affects Children's Learning*, 79.
8. Erdley and Dweck, "Children's Implicit Personality Theories as Predictors of Their Social Judgments," 863–878.
9. Langer, *Mindfulness*.

10. Alternatively, they were to imagine that their job was to solicit money from wealthy philanthropists, but that while driving to a meeting with one, they were in an accident in which their car wasn't badly damaged, but the other car was written off. The other driver turns out to be the philanthropist.

11. Giltay et al., "Dispositional Optimism and All-Cause and Cardiovascular Mortality in a Prospective Cohort of Elderly Dutch Men and Women," 1126–1135.

CHAPTER 4: "GOOD JOB!" FEEDBACK, PRAISE, AND OTHER RESPONSES

1. Found at http://thinkexist.com/quotations/praise/2.html.

2. Found at http://www.tentmaker.org/Quotes/flattery-criticism.htm.

3. Hattie, *Visible Learning: A Synthesis of over 800 Meta-Analyses Relating to Achievement*, 173. Hattie reminds us that "feedback is most powerful when it is from student to teacher, that is, when teachers are open to feedback from students, when they listen and observe closely."

4. Kamins and Dweck, "Person Versus Process Praise and Criticism: Implications for Contingent Self-Worth and Coping," 835–847. There are actually three groups in this study, but for simplicity only two are discussed here.

5. Ibid., 840.

6. Ibid.

7. Ibid., 838.

8. Cimpian et al., "Subtle Linguistic Cues Affect Children's Motivation," 314–316.

9. Ibid., 315.

10. Seligman and Nolen-Hoeksma, "Explanatory Style and Depression," 125–139.

11. http://fds.oup.com/www.oup.com/pdf/oxed/primary/rwi/RWIParentLetterApril2011.pdf.

12. There is no experimental evidence that I'm aware of to support the specific examples in this section. A good reference for praise more generally is Kohn, *Punished by Rewards: The Trouble with Gold Stars, Incentive Plans, A's, Praise, and Other Bribes*.

13. Horn and Giacobbe, *Talking, Drawing, Writing: Lessons for Our Youngest Writers*, 47–48.

14. McCloskey, "Taking on a Learning Disability: Negotiating Special Education and Learning to Read," 208.

15. Dweck, *Self-Theories: Their Role in Motivation, Personality, and Development*, 128.

16. Janeczko, *A Poke in the I: A Collection of Concrete Poems*.

17. Reilly, "Finding the Right Words: Art Conversations and Poetry," 103.

18. R. G. Williams and M. Williams, *Brothers in Hope: The Story of the Lost Boys of Sudan*; Wilkes, *One Day We Had to Run: Refugee Children Tell Their Stories in Words and Paintings*.

19. Troyer and Youngreen, "Conflict and Creativity in Groups," 409–427.

20. Some refer to this as "assessment for learning" (as opposed to assessment of learning), e.g., Black and Wiliam, "Assessment and Classroom Learning," 7–74.

CHAPTER 5: ANY OTHER WAYS TO THINK ABOUT THAT?
INQUIRY, DIALOGUE, UNCERTAINTY, AND DIFFERENCE

1. Langer, *Mindfulness*.

2. Nystrand, "Research on the Role of Classroom Discourse as It Affects Reading Comprehension," 400.

3. van den Branden, "Does Negotiation of Meaning Promote Reading Comprehension? A Study of Multilingual Primary School Classes," 426–443.

4. Saunders and Goldenberg, "Effects of Instructional Conversations and Literature Logs on Limited- and Fluent-English Proficient Students' Story Comprehension and Thematic Understanding," 4.

5. Nystrand et al., *Opening Dialogue: Understanding the Dynamics of Language and Learning in the English Classroom*.

6. Nichols, *Talking About Text: Guiding Students to Increase Comprehension Through Purposeful Talk*, 62–63. Some author annotations specific to Nichols's text have been edited out of the transcript to avoid confusion.

7. Burleigh, *Stealing Home: Jackie Robinson: Against the Odds*.

8. Yanoff, "Inquiry and Ideological Becoming in First Grade Literature Discussions."

9. Lindfors, *Children's Inquiry: Using Language to Make Sense of the World*, 137.

10. Quoted in an article by Garrison Keillor, "The Last Picture Show."

11. Thorkildsen, "The Way Tests Teach: Children's Theories of How Much Testing Is Fair in School," 61–79.

12. Davydov, "35 Weird Facts You Never Heard Of."

13. Olson, "Strange Things You Likely Didn't Know."

14. Langer, *Mindfulness*, 45.

15. Langer, "The Prevention of Mindlessness," 280–287.

16. Self-respect; I am not referring to self-esteem. See
Langer, "Self-Esteem vs. Self-Respect," 32.

17. Yanoff, "Inquiry and Ideological Becoming in First Grade Literature Discussions."

18. Berger, *Grandfather Twilight*.

19. Kruglanski and Webster, "Motivated Closing of the Mind: 'Seizing' and 'Freezing,'" 263.

20. Kruglanski, Webster, and Klem, "Motivated Resistance and Openness to Persuasion in the Presence or Absence of Prior Information," 861–876.

21. Lattimer, "Gaining Perspective: Recognizing the Processes by Which Students Come to Understand and Respect Alternative Viewpoints," 6–7.

22. Pierro et al., "Autocracy Bias in Informal Groups Under Need for Closure," 405–417.

23. Kruglanski et al., "Groups as Epistemic Providers: Need for Closure and the Unfolding of Group-Centrism," 84–100.

24. De Grada and Kruglanski, "Motivated Cognition and Group Interaction: Need for Closure Affects the Contents and Processes," 346.

25. Jost, Kruglanski, and Simon, "Effects of Epistemic Motivation on Conservatism, Intolerance and Other System-Justifying Attitudes," 91–116.

26. Turner and Killian, *Collective Behaviour*.

27. Shah, Kruglanski, and Thompson, "Membership Has Its (Epistemic) Rewards: Need for Closure Effects on In-Group Bias," 383–393.

28. Kruglanski et al., "When Similarity Breeds Content: Need for Closure and the Allure of Homogeneous and Self-Resembling Groups," 648–662.

29. Kruglanski and Webster, "Group Members' Reactions to Opinion Deviates and Conformists at Varying Degrees of Proximity to Decision Deadline and of Environmental Noise," 212–225.

30. Shah, Kruglanski, and Thompson, "Membership Has Its (Epistemic) Rewards: Need for Closure Effects on In-Group Bias," 383–393; Kosic et al., "Social Cognition of Immigrants' Acculturation: Effects of the Need for Closure and the Reference Group at Entry," 1–18.

31. Janis, *Groupthink: Psychological Studies of Policy Decisions and Fiascoes*.

32. Johnston and Backer, "Inquiry and a Good Conversation: 'I Learn a Lot from Them,'" 37–53.

33. Vygotsky, *Mind in Society: The Development of Higher Psychological Processes*.

34. Piaget, *The Moral Judgement of the Child*.

35. Browne, *Voices in the Park*.

36. Nichols, *Expanding Comprehension with Multigenre Text Sets*. For Kathy Short and her colleagues' work, see http://wowlit.org/.

37. Nystrand, "Research on the Role of Classroom Discourse as It Affects Reading Comprehension," 393–412.

CHAPTER 6: SOCIAL IMAGINATION

1. Lee, *To Kill a Mockingbird*, 30.

2. Vygotsky, *Mind in Society: The Development of Higher Psychological Processes*; Brooks, *The Social Animal: The Hidden Sources of Love, Character, and Achievement*.

3. Children deprived of human social contact in the early months of life frequently waste away. Those who survive suffer major psychological and physical damage.

Research on this anaclitic depression was first taken seriously by Renee Spitz. See Perry, *Born for Love: Why Empathy Is Essential—and Endangered.*

4. Nichols, *Comprehension Through Conversation: The Power of Purposeful Talk in the Reading Workshop,* 51, 67–68; Brisson, *The Summer My Father Was Ten.*

5. Almasi and Garas-York, "Comprehension and Discussion of Text," 470–493; Murphy et al., "Examining the Effects of Classroom Discussion on Students' Comprehension of Text: A Meta-Analysis," 740–764; Soter et al., "What the Discourse Tells Us: Talk and Indicators of High-Level Comprehension," 372–391.

6. Phillips, Baron-Cohen, and Rutter, "Can Children with Autism Understand Intentions?" 337–348.

7. Baron-Cohen et al., "The Reading the Mind in the Eyes Test Revised Version: A Study with Normal Adults, and Adults with Asperger Syndrome or High Functioning Autism," 241–251.

8. Sharp, "Theory of Mind and Conduct Problems in Children: Deficits in Reading the 'Emotions of the Eyes,'" 1149–1158.

9. Social imagination might be to social life what phonemic insight is to literacy. It allows insight into how things are related to one another.

10. One way of assessing this ability involves listening to stories and predicting the feelings, beliefs, intentions, and actions of the characters. For example, watching a little puppet play, children might be asked to predict what two characters believe about each other, given what has happened in the play. Alternatively, they might be asked which box Billy (a doll) will look under to find a toy that Billy watched being hidden in a red box, but which the observing child (but not Billy) knows has since been moved to the blue box. The task requires the child to hold both his own perspective and Billy's in mind at once. Other scenarios require quite complex reasoning about what different actors think about each other's motives, given what they know and given their perspectives.

11. Harris, "Conversation, Pretense, and Theory of Mind," 70–83; Lohmann, Tomasello, and Meyer, "Linguistic Communication and Social Understanding," 245–266.

12. Peskin and Astington, "The Effects of Adding Metacognitive Language to Story Texts," 253.

13. Caillies and Le Sourn-Bissaoui, "Children's Understanding of Idioms and Theory of Mind Development," 703–711.

14. Filippova and Astington, "Further Development in Social Reasoning Revealed in Discourse Irony Understanding," 126–138.

15. Baird and Astington, "The Role of Mental State Understanding in the Development of Moral Cognition and Moral Action," 37–49.

16. Watson et al., "Social Interaction Skills and Theory of Mind in Young Children," 386–391.

17. Lattimer, "Gaining Perspective: Recognizing the Processes by Which Students Come to Understand and Respect Alternative Viewpoints," 6.

18. Levy and Dweck, "Trait- Versus Process-Focused Social Judgment," 151–172.

19. Sodian, Hulsken, and Thoermer, "The Self and Action in Theory of Mind Research," 777.

20. Bernier, Carlson, and Whipple, "From External Regulation to Self-Regulation: Early Parenting Precursors of Young Children's Executive Functioning," 326–339.

21. Finkel et al., "High-Maintenance Interaction: Inefficient Social Coordination Impairs Self-Regulation," 456–475.

22. Fahie and Symons, "Executive Functioning and Theory of Mind in Children Clinically Referred for Attention and Behavior Problems," 51–73; Sodian, Hulsken, and Thoermer, "The Self and Action in Theory of Mind Research," 777; Soorya and Halpern, "Psychosocial Interventions for Motor Coordination, Executive Functions, and Socialization Deficits in ADHD and ASD," 48–54.

23. Centers for Disease Control and Prevention, "Key Findings: Trends in the Prevalence of Developmental Disabilities in U.S. Children, 1997–2008."

There are many potential or partial explanations for this increase, including increased sensitivity and acceptability of assessments, increased advertising by pharmaceutical companies, and so forth. However, there is reason to consider causes for which we have some constructive potential solutions.

24. Sharp, "Theory of Mind and Conduct Problems in Children: Deficits in Reading the 'Emotions of the Eyes,'" 1149–1158.
25. Mohr et al., "The Role of Perspective Taking in Anger Arousal," 507–517.
26. Baird and Astington, "The Role of Mental State Understanding in the Development of Moral Cognition and Moral Action," 37–49.
27. Coie and Dodge, "Aggression and Antisocial Behavior," 779–862.
28. Dodge, "Social Cognition and Children's Aggressive Behavior," 162–170; Graham, Hudley, and Williams, "Attributional and Emotional Determinants of Aggression Among African-American and Latino Young Adolescents," 731–740; Hudley, "Perceptions of Intentionality, Feelings of Anger, and Reactive Aggression," 39–56; Nasby, Hayden, and DePaulo, "Attributional Bias Among Aggressive Boys to Interpret Unambiguous Social Stimuli as Displays of Hostility," 459–468.
29. Halliday-Boykins and Graham, "At Both Ends of the Gun: Testing the Relationship Between Community Violence Exposure," 383; Schultz, Izard, and Ackerman, "Children's Anger Attribution Bias: Relations to Family Environment and Social Adjustment," 284–301; Sheeber et al., "Mothers' and Fathers' Attributions for Adolescent Behavior: An Examination in Families of Depressed, Subdiagnostic, and Nondepressed Youth," 871–881; Snyder et al., "The Contributions of Ineffective Discipline and Parental Hostile Attributions of Child Misbehavior to the Development of Conduct Problems at Home and School," 30–41.
30. Hudley, Graham, and Taylor, "Reducing Aggressive Behavior and Increasing Motivation in School: The Evolution of an Intervention to Strengthen School Adjustment," 251–260.
31. Understanding and sharing emotions and sensations—developing children's empathy tends to be passed on more through mothers. Expanding their ability to understand the beliefs and wishes in others tends to be passed on more through fathers.
32. Peterson and Siegal, "Insights into Theory of Mind from Deafness and Autism," 123.
33. Perner et al., "Exploration of the Autistic Child's Theory of Mind: Knowledge, Belief, and Communication," 689.
34. Hua et al., "The Effects of Theory-of-Mind and Social Skill Training on the Social Competence of a Sixth-Grade Student with Autism," 228–242.
35. Huijing, Yanjie, and Qi, "Talking About Others Facilitates Theory of Mind in Chinese Preschoolers," 1726–1736.
36. Furrow et al., "Mental Terms in Mothers' and Children's Speech: Similarities and Relationships," 617–631; Adrián, Clemente, and Villanueva, "Mothers' Use of Cognitive State Verbs in Picture-Book Reading and the Development of Children's Understanding of Mind: A Longitudinal Study," 1052–1067; Lysaker et al., "Reading and Social Imagination: What Relationally Oriented Instruction Can Do for Children."
37. Martin, *Snowflake Bentley*.
38. Boal, *Theatre of the Oppressed*.
39. Hudley, Graham, and Taylor, "Reducing Aggressive Behavior and Increasing Motivation in School: The Evolution of an Intervention to Strengthen School Adjustment," 251–260.
40. Sam Rayburn, quoted from the *Chicago Tribune*, "No one has a finer command of language than the person who keeps his mouth shut," in *The Week*, January 16, 2009, 17.

CHAPTER 7. MORAL AGENCY: MORAL DEVELOPMENT AND CIVIC ENGAGEMENT
1. Lattimer, "Gaining Perspective: Recognizing the Processes by Which Students Come to Understand and Respect Alternative Viewpoints."

2. Hahn, *Becoming Political: Comparative Perspectives on Citizenship Education*.

3. Cowhey, *Black Ants and Buddhists: Thinking Critically and Teaching Differently in the Primary Grades*, 132.

4. Huijing, Yanjie, and Qi, "Talking About Others Facilitates Theory of Mind in Chinese Preschoolers," 1726–1736.

5. Miller, Bersoff, and Harwood, "Perceptions of Social Responsibilities in India and in the United States: Moral Imperatives or Personal Decisions?" 33–47; Miller and Luthar, "Issues of Interpersonal Responsibility and Accountability: A Comparison of Indians' and Americans' Moral Judgments," 237–261.

6. Iyengar and Lepper, "Rethinking the Value of Choice: A Cultural Perspective on Intrinsic Motivation," 349–366.

7. Miller, "Culture and Agency: Implications for Psychological Theories of Motivation and Social Development," 59–99.

8. Langer, *The Power of Mindful Learning*.

9. The students' commitment to conservation in this classroom is, in part, a moral commitment to the children of the future, whom they do not know, but can imagine.

10. Galinsky and Moskowitz, "Perspective-Taking: Decreasing Stereotype Expression, Stereotype Accessibility, and In-Group Favoritism," 708–724.

11. Shih and Pittinsky, "Stereotype Susceptibility: Identity Salience and Shifts in Quantitative Performance," 80.

12. Ambady et al., "Stereotype Susceptibility in Children: Effects of Identity Activation on Quantitative Performance," 385.

13. Steele and Aronson, "Stereotype Threat and the Intellectual Test Performance of African-Americans," 797–811.

14. Aronson, Fried, and Good, "Reducing the Effects of Stereotype Threat on African American College Students by Shaping Theories of Intelligence," 113–125.

15. Chatard et al., "Performance Boosts in the Classroom: Stereotype Endorsement and Prejudice Moderate Stereotype Lift," 1421–1424.

16. S. P. Oliner and P. M. Oliner, *The Altruistic Personality: Rescuers of Jews in Nazi Europe*.

17. Eisenberg and Fabes, "Prosocial Development," 701–778.

18. Wentzel, "Student Motivation in Middle School: The Role of Perceived Pedagogical Caring," 411–419. Of course caring, as Wentzel's research points out, is demonstrated more by characteristics such as democratic classrooms— characteristics I describe throughout this book—than by overt statements like Jeralyn's. But then, as in Jeralyn's case, overt expressions are more likely to occur in that context.

19. Eisenberg and Fabes, "Prosocial Development," 701–778.

20. S. P. Oliner and P. M. Oliner, *The Altruistic Personality: Rescuers of Jews in Nazi Europe*.

21. Fabes et al., "Effects of Rewards on Children's Prosocial Motivation: A Socialization Study," 357–368.

22. Schweinhart and Weikart, "Why Curriculum Matters in Early Childhood Education," 57. The comparison also included a traditional nursery school. For brevity, and because the traditional nursery program outcomes fell between the other two, only the Direct Instruction vs. the High/Scope program are considered.

23. Schweinhart and Wallgren, "Effects of a Follow-Through Program on School Achievement," 43–56. For a more extensive listing of resources, see http://www.highscope.org/content.asp?contentid=219.

24. Schweinhart and Weikart, "The Advantages of High/Scope: Helping Children Lead Successful Lives," 76.

25. Schweinhart et al., *Lifetime Effects: The High/Scope Perry Preschool Study Through Age 40*.

26. For further financial analyses, see Nores et al., "Updating the Economic Impacts of the High/Scope Perry Preschool Program," 245–261.

27. Deci et al., "Effects of Performance Standards on Teaching Styles: Behavior of Controlling Teachers," 852–859; McNeil, *Contradictions of School Reform: Education Costs of Standardized Testing*; Rex and Nelson, "How Teachers' Professional Identities Position High-Stakes Test Preparation in Their Classrooms," 1288–1331; Sheppard, "The Hazards of High-Stakes Testing," 53.

28. Luthar and McMahon, "Peer Reputation Among Inner-City Adolescents: Structure and Correlates," 581–603.

CHAPTER 8: THINKING TOGETHER, WORKING TOGETHER

1. Found at http://www.brainyquote.com/quotes/authors/c/charles_darwin.html.

2. D. W. Johnson and R. Johnson, "An Educational Psychology Success Story: Social Interdependence Theory and Cooperative Learning," 365–379.

3. Vygotsky, *Mind in Society: The Development of Higher Psychological Processes*.

4. Mercer, Wegerif, and Dawes, "Children's Talk and the Development of Reasoning in the Classroom," 95–111.

5. Ibid., 103.

6. Ibid., 104.

7. Ibid.

8. Darnon et al., "Mastery and Performance Goals Predict Epistemic and Relational Conflict Regulation," 766–776.

9. Woolley et al., "Evidence for a Collective Intelligence Factor in the Performance of Human Groups," 686–688.

10. Boaler, "Promoting Relational Equity: The Mixed Ability Mathematics Approach That Taught Students High Levels of Responsibility, Respect, and Thought," 167–194; Osborne and Chin, "The Role of Discourse in Learning Science," 88–102; Solomon, *Mathematical Literacy: Developing Identities of Inclusion*; Wegerif, *Dialogic Education and Technology: Expanding the Space of Learning*; Yackel, Cobb, and Wood, "Small Group Interactions as a Source of Learning Opportunities in Second-Grade Mathematics," 390–408.

11. Trickey and Topping, "'Philosophy for Children': A Systematic Review," 365–380.

12. Trickey and Topping, "Collaborative Philosophical Enquiry for School Children," 599–614; Topping and Trickey, "Collaborative Philosophical Enquiry for School Children: Cognitive Effects at 10–12 Years," 271–288.

13. Topping and Trickey, "Collaborative Philosophical Inquiry for Schoolchildren: Cognitive Gains at 2-Year Follow-Up," 787–796.

14. Mercer, Wegerif, and Dawes, "Children's Talk and the Development of Reasoning in the Classroom," 95–111.

15. Ting et al., "Collaborative Reasoning in China and Korea," 400–424. Argumentation strategies and their development are, of course, critical for mathematics and science. See, for example, Schwarz, Prusak, and Hershkowitz, "Argumentation and Mathematics," 103–127.

16. Giff, *Ronald Morgan Goes to Bat*; Munsch, *The Paper Bag Princess*; Steig, *Doctor De Soto*.

17. Lattimer, "Gaining Perspective: Recognizing the Processes by Which Students Come to Understand and Respect Alternative Viewpoints."

18. Ting et al., "Collaborative Reasoning in China and Korea," 400–424. The full introduction was this:

> *Ms. Dong: We are going to hold altogether four discussions about four stories. This is our first one. Each time after you finish reading the story, I will propose a question. There is no fixed answer to this question. That is to say, you may have different opinions about it. You can speak freely without raising your hand, but please don't interrupt others while they are talking. Listen respectfully to everyone's ideas. The discussion will be yours. I am only going to start it and then it will be your responsibility to make the discussion go well. If we find somebody is too silent, we can invite him or her into the discussion. As I've already mentioned, it is fine for you*

guys to have different opinions, and I appreciate that. Our question today is, Should Doctor De Soto let in the fox for tooth replacement the next day? [Five seconds of silence]

Ms. Dong: You don't have to look at me when you talk. Just look at each other among yourselves.

Notice that the introduction touches on all the necessary points of civil dialogue. However, the students also had something interesting and provocative to discuss.

19. Cowhey, *Black Ants and Buddhists: Thinking Critically and Teaching Differently in the Primary Grades*, 90–91.
20. Burbules, *Dialogue in Teaching: Theory and Practice.*
21. Nichols, *Talking About Text: Guiding Students to Increase Comprehension Through Purposeful Talk.*
22. Darnon, Butera, and Harackiewicz, "Achievement Goals in Social Interactions: Learning with Mastery vs. Performance Goals," 61–70.
23. Darnon, Doll, and Butera, "Dealing with a Disagreeing Partner: Relational and Epistemic Conflict Elaboration," 227–242.
24. Nichols, *Talking About Text: Guiding Students to Increase Comprehension Through Purposeful Talk*, 104–105.
25. Mercer, Wegerif, and Dawes, "Children's Talk and the Development of Reasoning in the Classroom," 95–111.
26. Johnston and Backer, "Inquiry and a Good Conversation: 'I Learn a Lot from Them,'" 37–53.
27. D. W. Johnson and R. Johnson, "An Educational Psychology Success Story: Social Interdependence Theory and Cooperative Learning," 365–379.
28. D. W. Johnson and R. Johnson, "Building Friendships Between Handicapped and Nonhandicapped Students: Effects of Cooperative and Individualistic Instruction," 415–424; D. W. Johnson and R. Johnson, "Effects of Cooperative and Individualistic Learning Experiences on Interethnic Interaction," 454–459; D. W. Johnson and R. Johnson, "Effects of Cooperative and Individualistic Instruction on Handicapped and Nonhandicapped Students," 257–268.
29. Wentzel, "Relations of Social Goal Pursuit to Social Acceptance, Classroom Behavior, and Perceived Social Support," 173–182.
30. D. W. Johnson and R. Johnson, "An Educational Psychology Success Story: Social Interdependence Theory and Cooperative Learning," 365–379.
31. Finkel et al., "High-Maintenance Interaction: Inefficient Social Coordination Impairs Self-Regulation," 456–475.
32. Volet, Vauras, and Salonen, "Self- and Social Regulation in Learning Contexts: An Integrative Perspective," 215–226.
33. Gilmore, "Large-Scale Assessment and Teachers' Assessment Capacity: Learning Opportunities for Teachers in the National Education Monitoring Project in New Zealand," 343–361.

CHAPTER 9: CHOICE WORLDS

1. Aikin, *The Story of the Eight-Year Study.*
2. R. Bomer and K. Bomer, *For a Better World: Reading and Writing for Social Action*, 157.
3. Peterson, Park, and Seligman, "Orientations to Happiness and Life Satisfaction: The Full Life Versus the Empty Life," 25–41.
4. White House, "Education: Guiding Principles."
5. McCollister, French, and Fang, "The Cost of Crime to Society: New Crime-Specific Estimates for Policy and Program Evaluation," 98–109.
I do not want to suggest that teachers can simply overcome all the effects of societal factors such as poverty. However, children educated in this manner, as adults, would be more likely to work to eliminate poverty and other inequities and more likely to educate than incarcerate.

6. Kingsbury, "Tallying Mental Illness' Costs."

7. Diener et al., "Dispositional Affect and Job Outcomes," 229–259.

8. Peterson, Park, and Seligman, "Orientations to Happiness and Life Satisfaction: The Full Life Versus the Empty Life," 25–41.

9. Stojanovich and Marisavljevich, "Stress as a Trigger of Autoimmune Disease," 209–213.

10. Lyubomirsky, King, and Diener, "The Benefits of Frequent Positive Affect: Does Happiness Lead to Success?" 803–855.

11. Tyrese Reed, one of Jeralyn Johnson's fourth-grade students.

12. Carr and Claxton, "Tracking the Development of Learning Dispositions," 9–37.

13. Ibid., 11.

14. Josephson Institute, "The Ethics of American Youth: 2010."

15. Charney, *Teaching Children to Care: Classroom Management for Ethical and Academic Growth, K–8*, 312–313.

16. Aikin, *The Story of the Eight-Year Study*.
    See the complete series documenting this study, including:
    Giles, McCutchen, and Zechiel, *Exploring the Curriculum: The Work of the Thirty Schools from the Viewpoint of Curriculum Consultants*; Smith, Tyler, and the Evaluation Staff, *Appraising and Recording Student Progress*; Chamberlin et al., *Did They Succeed in College? The Follow-Up Study of the Graduates of the Thirty Schools*; *Thirty Schools Tell Their Story: Each School Writes of Its Participation in the Eight-Year Study*.

17. The idea that each person should individually be the complete Renaissance person is an absurdity we nurture to imagine equity in a competitive, individualistic society.

18. Equalizing average achievement across race, class, gender, language, culture, and any other historical or contextual hurdles will, it is believed, indicate a just society. Provided we ignore obvious impediments, such as the complexities of poverty, the limited number of well-paying jobs, and the likelihood of everyone becoming similarly competent at everything, this is an admirable goal.

19. Ivey and Johnston, "Reading Engagement, Achievement, and Moral Development in Adolescence."

20. Ibid., 9–10.

21. Beah, *A Long Way Gone: Memoirs of a Boy Soldier*.

22. Ivey and Johnston, "Reading Engagement, Achievement, and Moral Development in Adolescence," 6–7.

23. Flanagan and Stout, "Developmental Patterns of Social Trust Between Early and Late Adolescence: Age and School Climate Effects," 748–773.

24. Ivey and Johnston, "Transcending the Curriculum and Other Consequences of Engaged Reading on Adolescent Learners."

25. We have enforceable societal rules to ensure that we have a safe and equitable society. But whether people come to understand these rules as impediments to their own free choice or as fair management of collective and conflicting choice is another matter.

26. People like Mary Cowhey (see her book, *Black Ants and Buddhists*); Kathy Short's work (http://wowlit.org/on-line-publications/stories/storiesi2/) and Rethinking Schools (http://www.rethinkingschools.org/index.shtml).

27. Nichols, *Comprehension Through Conversation: The Power of Purposeful Talk in the Reading Workshop*, 77.

28. Ibid., 87.

Bibliography

Adrián, J. E., R. A. Clemente, and L. Villanueva. 2007. "Mothers' Use of Cognitive State Verbs in Picture-Book Reading and the Development of Children's Understanding of Mind: A Longitudinal Study." *Child Development* 78(4): 1052–1067.

Aikin, W. 1942. *The Story of the Eight-Year Study*. New York: Harper. http://www.8yearstudy.org/index.html.

Almasi, J. F., and K. Garas-York. 2009. "Comprehension and Discussion of Text." In *Handbook of Research on Reading Comprehension*, eds. S. E. Israel and G. G. Duffy. New York: Routledge.

Ambady, N., M. Shih, A. Kim, and T. L. Pittinsky. 2001. "Stereotype Susceptibility in Children: Effects of Identity Activation on Quantitative Performance." *Psychological Science* 12(5): 385.

Aronson, J., C. Fried, and C. Good. 2002. "Reducing the Effects of Stereotype Threat on African American College Students by Shaping Theories of Intelligence." *Journal of Experimental Social Psychology* 38: 113–125.

Baer, A. R., H. Grant, and C. S. Dweck. 2005. "Personal Goals, Dysphoria, and Coping Strategies." Unpublished manuscript, Columbia University. Cited in D. C. Molden and C. S. Dweck. 2006. "Finding 'Meaning' in Psychology." *American Psychologist* 61(3): 192–203.

Baird, G. L., W. D. Scott, E. Dearing, and S. K. Hamill. 2009. "Cognitive Self-Regulation in Youth with and Without Learning Disabilities: Academic Self-Efficacy, Theories of Intelligence, Learning vs. Performance Goal Preferences, and Effort Attributions." *Journal of Social & Clinical Psychology* 28(7): 881–908.

Baird, J. A., and J. W. Astington. 2004. "The Role of Mental State Understanding in the Development of Moral Cognition and Moral Action." *New Directions for Child & Adolescent Development* 103: 37–49.

Baron-Cohen, S., S. Wheelwright, J. Hill, Y. Raste, and I. Plumb. 2001. "The Reading the Mind in the Eyes Test Revised Version: A Study with Normal Adults, and Adults with Asperger Syndrome or High-Functioning Autism." *Journal of Child Psychology and Psychiatry* 42(2): 241–251.

Beah, I. 2007. *A Long Way Gone: Memoirs of a Boy Soldier*. New York: Farrar, Straus and Giroux.

Berger, B. H. 1984. *Grandfather Twilight*. New York: Philomel.

Bernier, A., S. M. Carlson, and N. Whipple. 2010. "From External Regulation to Self-Regulation: Early Parenting Precursors of Young Children's Executive Functioning." *Child Development* 81(1): 326–339.

Black, P., and D. Wiliam. 1998. "Assessment and Classroom Learning." *Assessment in Education: Principles, Policy & Practice* 5(1): 7–74. doi: 10.1080/0969595980050102.

Blackwell, L. S., K. H. Trzesniewski, C. S. Dweck. 2007. "Implicit Theories of Intelligence Predict Achievement Across an Adolescent Transition: A Longitudinal Study and an Intervention." *Child Development* 78(1): 246–263.

Boal, A. 1979. *Theatre of the Oppressed.* Trans C. A. McBride and M. O. McBride. New York: Theatre Communications Group.

Boaler, J. 2008. "Promoting Relational Equity: The Mixed Ability Mathematics Approach That Taught Students High Levels of Responsibility, Respect, and Thought." *British Educational Research Journal* 34(2): 167–194.

Bomer, R., and K. Bomer. 2001. *For a Better World: Reading and Writing for Social Action.* Portsmouth, NH: Heinemann.

Brisson, P. 1998. *The Summer My Father Was Ten.* Honesdale, PA: Boyds Mills.

Brooks, D. 2011. *The Social Animal: The Hidden Sources of Love, Character, and Achievement.* New York: Random House.

Browne, A. 2001. *Voices in the Park.* New York: DK.

Burbules, N. 1993. *Dialogue in Teaching: Theory and Practice.* New York: Teachers College.

Burleigh, R. 2007. *Stealing Home: Jackie Robinson: Against the Odds.* New York: Simon and Schuster.

Caillies, S. P., and S. Le Sourn-Bissaoui. 2008. "Children's Understanding of Idioms and Theory of Mind Development." *Developmental Science* 11(5): 703–711.

Carr, M., and G. Claxton. 2002. "Tracking the Development of Learning Dispositions." *Assessment in Education* 9(1): 9–37.

Cazden, C. 2008. "Reflections on the Study of Classroom Talk." In *Exploring Talk in Schools: Inspired by the Work of Douglas Barnes*, eds. N. Mercer and S. Hodgkinson. London: Sage.

Centers for Disease Control and Prevention. 2011. "Key Findings: Trends in the Prevalence of Developmental Disabilities in U.S. Children, 1997–2008." http://www.cdc.gov/ncbddd/features/birthdefects-dd-keyfindings.html.

Chamberlin, D., E. S. Chamberlin, N. E. Drought, and W. E. Scott. 1942. *Did They Succeed in College? The Follow-Up Study of the Graduates of the Thirty Schools.* New York: Harper and Brothers.

Charney, R. S. 2002. *Teaching Children to Care: Classroom Management for Ethical and Academic Growth, K–8.* Rev. ed. Turners Falls, MA: Northeast Foundation for Children.

Chatard, A., L. Selimbegovic, P. Konan, and G. Mugny. 2008. "Performance Boosts in the Classroom: Stereotype Endorsement and Prejudice Moderate Stereotype Lift." *Journal of Experimental Social Psychology* 44(5): 1421–1424.

Chiu, C., C. S. Dweck, J. Y. Tong, and J. H. Fu. 1997. "Implicit Theories and Conceptions of Morality." *Journal of Personality and Social Psychology* 3: 923–940.

Cimpian, A., H. M. Arce, E. M. Markman, and C. S. Dweck. 2007. "Subtle Linguistic Cues Affect Children's Motivation." *Psychological Science* 18(4): 314–316.

Clay, Marie. 1993. *Reading Recovery: A Guidebook for Teachers in Training.* Portsmouth, NH: Heinemann.

Coie, J., and K. Dodge. 1998. "Aggression and Antisocial Behavior." In *Handbook of Child Psychology: Social, Emotional, and Personality Development.* 5th ed. Vol. 3, ed. N. Eisenberg, 779–862. New York: Wiley.

Cowhey, M. 2006. *Black Ants and Buddhists: Thinking Critically and Teaching Differently in the Primary Grades.* Portland, ME: Stenhouse.

Cury, F., D. Da Fonseca, A. C. Moller, and A. J. Elliot. 2006. "The Social-Cognitive Model of Achievement Motivation and the 2 × 2 Achievement Goal Framework." *Journal of Personality and Social Psychology* 90(4): 666–679. doi: 10.1037/0022-3514.90.4.666.

Darnon, C. L., F. Butera, and J. M. Harackiewicz. 2007. "Achievement Goals in Social Interactions: Learning with Mastery vs. Performance Goals." *Motivation & Emotion* 31(1): 61–70.

Darnon, C. L., S. B. Doll, and F. Butera. 2007. "Dealing with a Disagreeing Partner: Relational and Epistemic Conflict Elaboration." *European Journal of Psychology of Education* 22(3): 227–242.

Darnon, C. L., D. Muller, S. M. Schrager, N. Pannuzzo, and F. Butera, "Mastery and Performance Goals Predict Epistemic and Relational Conflict Regulation." *Journal of Educational Psychology* 98(4): 766–776.

Davydov, D. 2007. "35 Weird Facts You Never Heard Of." Madconomist.com. http://madconomist.com/35-weird-facts-you-never-heard-of.

Deci, E. L., N. H. Siegel, R. M. Ryan, R. Koestner, and M. Kauffman. 1982. "Effects of Performance Standards on Teaching Styles: Behavior of Controlling Teachers." *Journal of Educational Psychology* 74: 852–859.

De Grada, E., and A. W. Kruglanski. 1999. "Motivated Cognition and Group Interaction: Need for Closure Affects the Contents and Processes." *Journal of Experimental Social Psychology* 35(4): 346.

Delizonna, L. L., R. P. Williams, and E. J. Langer. 2009. "The Effect of Mindfulness on Heart Rate Control." *Journal of Adult Development* 16(2): 61–65.

Diener, C. I., and C. S. Dweck. 1978. "An Analysis of Learned Helplessness: Continuous Changes in Performance, Strategy, and Achievement Cognitions Following Failure." *Journal of Personality and Social Psychology* 36(5): 451–462. doi: 10.1037/0022-3514.36.5.451.

———. 1980. "An Analysis of Learned Helplessness: II. The Processing of Success." *Journal of Personality and Social Psychology* 39(5): 940–952. doi: 10.1037/0022-3514.39.5.940.

Diener, E., C. Nickerson, R. E. Lucas, and E. Sandvik. 2002. "Dispositional Affect and Job Outcomes." *Social Indicators Research* 59: 229–259.

Dodge, K. 1980. "Social Cognition and Children's Aggressive Behavior." *Child Development* 51: 162–170.

Dong, T., R. C. Anderson, K. Il-Hee, and L. Yuan. 2008. "Collaborative Reasoning in China and Korea." *Reading Research Quarterly* 43(4): 400–424.

Dweck, C. S. 2000. *Self-Theories: Their Role in Motivation, Personality, and Development.* Philadelphia, PA: Psychology Press.

———. 2006. *Mindset: The New Psychology of Success.* New York: Random House.

Dweck, C. S., and E. L. Leggett. 1988. "A Social-Cognitive Approach to Motivation and Personality." *Psychological Review* 95: 256–273.

Eisenberg, N., and R. A. Fabes. 1998. "Prosocial Development." In *The Handbook of Child Psychology: Social, Emotional, and Personality Development.* 5th ed. Vol. 3, ed. N. Eisenberg, 701–778. New York: Wiley.

Erdley, C. A., and C. S. Dweck. 1993. "Children's Implicit Personality Theories as predictors of Their Social Judgments." *Child Development* 64(3): 863–878.

Fabes, R. A., J. Fultz, N. Eisenberg, T. May-Plumlee, and F. S. Christopher. 1989. "Effects of Rewards on Children's Prosocial Motivation: A Socialization Study." *Developmental Psychology* 62: 357–368.

Fahie, C. M., and D. K. Symons. "Executive Functioning and Theory of Mind in Children Clinically Referred for Attention and Behavior Problems." *Journal of Applied Developmental Psychology* 24(1): 51–73. doi: 10.1016/s0193-3973(03)00024-8.

Filippova, E., and J. W. Astington. 2008. "Further Development in Social Reasoning Revealed in Discourse Irony Understanding." *Child Development* 79(1): 126–138.

Finkel, E. J., W. K. Campbell, A. B. Brunell, A. N. Dalton, S. J. Scarbeck, and T. L. Chartrand. 2006. "High-Maintenance Interaction: Inefficient Social Coordination Impairs Self Regulation." *Journal of Personality and Social Psychology* 91(3): 456–475. doi: 10.1037/0022-3514.91.3.456.

Flanagan, C. A., and M. Stout. 2010. "Developmental Patterns of Social Trust Between Early and Late Adolescence: Age and School Climate Effects." *Journal of Research on Adolescence* 20(3): 748–773.

Furrow, D., C. Moore, J. Davidge, and L. Chiasson. 1992. "Mental Terms in Mothers' and Children's Speech: Similarities and Relationships." *Journal of Child Language* 19: 617–631.

Galinsky, A. D., and G. B. Moskowitz. 2000. "Perspective-Taking: Decreasing Stereotype Expression, Stereotype Accessibility, and In-Group Favoritism." *Journal of Personality and Social Psychology* 78(4): 708–724.

Giff, P. R. 1990. *Ronald Morgan Goes to Bat.* New York: Puffin.

Giles, H. H., S. P. McCutchen, and A. N. Zechiel. 1942. *Exploring the Curriculum: The Work of the Thirty Schools from the Viewpoint of Curriculum Consultants.* New York: Harper and Brothers.

Gilmore, A. 2002. "Large-Scale Assessment and Teachers' Assessment Capacity: Learning Opportunities for Teachers in the National Education Monitoring Project in New Zealand." *Assessment in Education: Principles, Policy & Practice* 9(3): 343–361.

Giltay, E. J., J. M. Geleijnse, F. G. Zitman, T. Hoekstra, and E. G. Schouten. 2004. "Dispositional Optimism and All-Cause and Cardiovascular Mortality in a Prospective Cohort of Elderly Dutch Men and Women." *Archives of General Psychiatry* 61: 1126–1135.

Graham, S., C. Hudley, and E. Williams. 1992. "Attributional and Emotional Determinants of Aggression Among African-American and Latino Young Adolescents." *Developmental Psychology* 28: 731–740.

Grant, H., and C. S. Dweck. 2003. "Clarifying Achievement Goals and Their Impact." *Journal of Personality and Social Psychology* 85(3): 541–553.

Hahn, C. L. 1998. *Becoming Political: Comparative Perspectives on Citizenship Education.* Albany: State University of New York.

Halliday, M. A. K. 1993. "Towards a Language-Based Theory of Learning." *Linguistics and Education* 5: 93–116.

Halliday-Boykins, C. A., and S. Graham. 2001. "At Both Ends of the Gun: Testing the Relationship Between Community Violence Exposure." *Journal of Abnormal Child Psychology* 29(5): 383.

Harris, P. L. 2005. "Conversation, Pretense, and Theory of Mind." In *Why Language Matters for Theory of Mind*, eds. J. W. Astington and J. A. Baird. Oxford, UK: Oxford University Press.

Hattie, J. A. C. 2009. *Visible Learning: A Synthesis of over 800 Meta-Analyses Relating to Achievement.* New York: Routledge.

Heyman, G. D., and C. S. Dweck. 1998. "Children's Thinking About Traits: Implications for Judgments of the Self and Others." *Child Development* 64(2): 391–403.

Hong, Y.-y., C.-y. Chiu, C. S. Dweck, D. M.-S. Lin, and W. Wan. 1999. "Implicit Theories, Attributions, and Coping: A Meaning System Approach." *Journal of Personality and Social Psychology* 77(3): 588–599.

Horn, M., and M. E. Giacobbe. 2007. *Talking, Drawing, Writing: Lessons for Our Youngest Writers.* Portland, ME: Stenhouse.

Hua, F., L. Ya-yu, T. Shuling, and G. Cartledge. 2008. "The Effects of Theory-of-Mind and Social Skill Training on the Social Competence of a Sixth-Grade Student with Autism." *Journal of Positive Behavior Interventions* 10(4): 228–242.

Hudley, C. 1994. "Perceptions of Intentionality, Feelings of Anger, and Reactive Aggression." In *Anger, Hostility, and Aggression: Assessment, Prevention, and Intervention Strategies for Youth*, eds. M. Furlong and D. Smith. Brandon, VT: Clinical Psychology.

Hudley, C., S. Graham, and A. Taylor. 2007. "Reducing Aggressive Behavior and Increasing Motivation in School: The Evolution of an Intervention to Strengthen School Adjustment." *Educational Psychologist* 42(4): 251–260.

Huijing, L., S. Yanjie, W. Qi. 2008. "Talking About Others Facilitates Theory of Mind in Chinese Preschoolers." *Developmental Psychology* 44(6): 1726–1736.

Ivey, G., and P. Johnston. 2010. "Reading Engagement, Achievement, and Moral Development in Adolescence." Paper presented at the annual meeting of the Literacy Research Association, Fort Worth, TX, December 2.

———. 2011. "Transcending the Curriculum and Other Consequences of Engaged Reading on Adolescent Learners." Presentation at the annual meeting of the International Reading Association, Orlando, FL, May 11.

Iyengar, S. S., and M. R. Lepper. 1999. "Rethinking the Value of Choice: A Cultural Perspective on Intrinsic Motivation." *Journal of Personality and Social Psychology* 76: 349–366.

Janeczko, P. B., ed. 2001. *A Poke in the I: A Collection of Concrete Poems.* Cambridge, MA: Candlewick.

Janis, I. L. 1982. *Groupthink: Psychological Studies of Policy Decisions and Fiascoes.* Boston: Houghton Mifflin.

Johnson, D. W., and R. Johnson. 1981a. "Building Friendships Between Handicapped and Nonhandicapped Students: Effects of Cooperative and Individualistic Instruction." *American Educational Research Journal* 18: 415–424.

———. 1981b. "Effects of Cooperative and Individualistic Learning Experiences on Interethnic Interaction." *Journal of Educational Psychology* 73: 454–459.

———. 1982. "Effects of Cooperative and Individualistic Instruction on Handicaped and Nonhandicapped Students." *Journal of Social Psychology* 118: 257–268.

———. 2009. "An Educational Psychology Success Story: Social Interdependence Theory and Cooperative Learning." *Educational Researcher* 38(5): 365–379.

Johnston, P. 2004. *Choice Words: How Our Language Affects Children's Learning.* Portland, ME: Stenhouse.

Johnston, P., and J. Backer. 2002. "Inquiry and a Good Conversation: 'I Learn a Lot from Them.'" In *Reading to Learn: Lessons from Exemplary Fourth-Grade Classrooms,* eds. R. L. Allington and P. H. Johnston. New York: Guilford.

Johnston, P., and K. Champeau. 2008. "High Stakes Testing: Narratives of the Cost of 'Friendly Fire.'" Presentation at the National Reading Conference, Orlando, FL, December 5.

Johnston, P., V. Goatley, and C. Dozier. 2008. "Educator Decision-Making Orientation." Presentation at the National Reading Conference, Orlando, FL, December 5.

Josephson Institute. 2010. "The Ethics of American Youth: 2010." Josephson Institute. http://charactercounts.org/programs/reportcard/2010/installment01_report-card _bullying-youth-violence.html.

Jost, J. T., A. W. Kruglanski, and L. Simon. 1999. "Effects of Epistemic Motivation on Conservatism, Intolerance and Other System-Justifying Attitudes." In *Shared Cognition in Organizations: The Management of Knowledge,* eds. L. I. Thompson, J. M. Levine, and D. M. Messick. Mahwah, NJ: Erlbaum.

Kamins, M. L., and C. S. Dweck. 1999. "Person Versus Process Praise and Criticism: Implications for Contingent Self-Worth and Coping." *Developmental Psychology* 35(3): 835–847.

Keillor, Garrison. 2007. "The Last Picture Show." *The Guardian,* January 3. http://www.guardian.co.uk/film/2007/jan/03/2.

Kingsbury, K. 2008. "Tallying Mental Illness' Costs." *Time,* May 9. http://www.time .com/time/health/article/0,8599,1738804,00.html#ixzz1ag51dKoq.

Knee, C. R. 1998. "Implicit Theories of Relationships: Assessment and Prediction of Romantic Relationship Initiation, Coping and Longevity." *Journal of Personality and Social Psychology* 74(2): 360–370.

Kohn, A. 1993. *Punished by Rewards: The Trouble with Gold Stars, Incentive Plans, A's, Praise, and Other Bribes.* New York: Houghton Mifflin.

Kosic, A., A. W. Kruglanski, A. Pierro, and L. Mannetti. 2004. "Social Cognition of Immigrants' Acculturation: Effects of the Need for Closure and the Reference Group at Entry." *Journal of Personality and Social Psychology* 86: 1–18.

Kruglanski, A. W., and D. M. Webster. 1991. "Group Members' Reactions to Opinion Deviates and Conformists at Varying Degrees of Proximity to Decision Deadline and of Environmental Noise." *Journal of Personality and Social Psychology* 61: 212–225.

———. 1996. "Motivated Closing of the Mind: 'Seizing' and 'Freezing.'" *Psychological Review* 103(2): 263.

Kruglanski, A. W., D. M. Webster, and A. Klem. 1993. "Motivated Resistance and Openness to Persuasion in the Presence or Absence of Prior Information." *Journal of Personality and Social Psychology* 65(5): 861–876.

Kruglanski, A. W., A. Pierro, L. Mannetti, and E. De Grada. 2006. "Groups as Epistemic Providers: Need for Closure and the Unfolding of Group Centrism." *Psychological Review* 113(1): 84–100.

Kruglanski, A. W., J. Y. Shah, A. Pierro, and L. Mannetti. 2002. "When Similarity Breeds Content: Need for Closure and the Allure of Homogeneous and Self-Resembling Groups." *Journal of Personality and Social Psychology* 83(3): 648–662.

Laczynski, A. R. 2006. "The Children Left Behind: Memories of Promoting Literacy." *Language Arts* 83(5): 395–403.

Langer, E. 1987. "The Prevention of Mindlessness." *Journal of Personality and Social Psychology* 53(2): 280–287.

———. 1989. *Mindfulness*. Reading, MA: Addison-Wesley.

———. 1997. *The Power of Mindful Learning*. Reading, MA: Addison-Wesley.

———. 1999. "Self-Esteem vs. Self-Respect." *Psychology Today*, November 1, 32.

Lattimer, H. 2009. "Gaining Perspective: Recognizing the Processes by Which Students Come to Understand and Respect Alternative Viewpoints." Presentation at the annual meeting of the American Educational Research Association. San Diego, CA, April.

Lee, H. 1962. *To Kill a Mockingbird*. New York: Grand Central.

Levy, S. R., and C. S. Dweck. 2005. "Trait- Versus Process-Focused Social Judgment." *Social Cognition* 16(1): 151–172.

Levy, S. R., J. E. Plaks, Y.-y. Hong, C.-y. Chiu, and C. S. Dweck. 2001. "Static Versus Dynamic Theories and the Perception of Groups: Different Routes to Different Destinations." *Personality and Social Psychology Review* 5(2): 156–168.

Levy-Tossman, I., A. Kaplan, and A. Assor. 2007. "Academic Goal Orientations, Multiple Goal Profiles, and Friendship Intimacy Among Early Adolescents." *Contemporary Educational Psychology* 32(2): 231–252.

Lindfors, J. W. 1999. *Children's Inquiry: Using Language to Make Sense of the World*. New York: Teachers College.

Lohmann, H., M. Tomasello, and S. Meyer. 2005. "Linguistic Communication and Social Imagination." In *Why Language Matters for Theory of Mind*, eds. J. W. Astington and J. A. Baird. Oxford, UK: Oxford University Press.

Luthar, S. S., and T. J. McMahon. 1996. "Peer Reputation Among Inner-City Adolescents: Structure and Correlates." *Journal of Research on Adolescence* 6(4): 581–603.

Lysaker, J., C. Tonge, D. Gauson, and A. Miller. 2009. "Relationally Oriented Reading Instruction and the Development of Listening Comprehension, Narrative Competence, and Social Imagination in 2nd and 3rd Grade Children." Paper presented at the National Reading Conference, Albuquerque, NM, December.

Lysaker, J. T., C. Tonge, D. Gauson, and A. Miller. Forthcoming. "Reading and Social Imagination: What Relationally Oriented Instruction Can Do for Children." *Reading Psychology*.

Lyubomirsky, S., L. King, and E. Diener. 2005. "The Benefits of Frequent Positive Affect: Does Happiness Lead to Success?" *Psychological Bulletin* 131(6): 803–855. doi: 10.1037/0033-2909.131.6.803.

Martin, J. B. 1998. *Snowflake Bentley*. Boston: Houghton Mifflin.

McCloskey, E. 2007. "Taking on a Learning Disability: Negotiating Special Education and Learning to Read." PhD diss., University at Albany-SUNY.

McCollister, K. E., M. T. French, and H. Fang. 2010. "The Cost of Crime to Society: New Crime-Specific Estimates for Policy and Program Evaluation." *Drug and Alcohol Dependence* 108(1/2): 98–109.

McNeil, L. M. 2000. *Contradictions of School Reform: Education Costs of Standardized Testing*. New York: Routledge.

Mercer, N., R. Wegerif, and L. Dawes. 1999. "Children's Talk and the Development of Reasoning in the Classroom." *British Educational Research Journal* 25(1): 95–111.

Miller, J. G. 2003. "Culture and Agency: Implications for Psychological Theories of Motivation and Social Development." In *Crosscultural Differences in Perspectives on the Self*, eds. V. Murphy-Berman and J. Berman. Lincoln: University of Nebraska Press.

Miller, J. G., D. M. Bersoff, and R. L. Harwood. 1990. "Perceptions of Social Responsibilities in India and in the United States: Moral Imperatives or Personal Decisions?" *Journal of Personality and Social Psychology* 58(1): 33–47.

Miller, J. G., and S. Luthar. 1989. "Issues of Interpersonal Responsibility and Accountability: A Comparison of Indians' and Americans' Moral Judgments." *Social Cognition* 7(3): 237–261.

Mohr, P., K. Howells, A. Gerace, A. Day, and M. Wharton. 2007. "The Role of Perspective Taking in Anger Arousal." *Personality and Individual Differences* 43(3): 507–517.

Molden, D. C., and C. S. Dweck. 2006. "Finding 'meaning' in psychology.'" *American Psychologist* 61(3): 192–203.

Munsch, R. N. 1999. *The Paper Bag Princess*. Buffalo, NY: Firefly.

Murphy, P. K., I. A. G. Wilkinson, A. O. Soter, M. N. Hennessey, and J. F. Alexander. 2009. "Examining the Effects of Classroom Discussion on Students' Comprehension of Text: A Meta-Analysis." *Journal of Educational Psychology* 101(3): 740–764.

Nasby, W., B. Hayden, and B. DePaulo. 1980. "Attributional Bias Among Aggressive Boys to Interpret Unambiguous Social Stimuli as Displays of Hostility." *Journal of Abnormal Psychology* 89: 459–468.

Nichols, M. 2006. *Comprehension Through Conversation: The Power of Purposeful Talk in the Reading Workshop*. Portsmouth, NH: Heinemann.

———. 2008. *Talking About Text: Guiding Students to Increase Comprehension Through Purposeful Talk*. Huntington Beach, CA: Shell Education.

———. 2009. *Expanding Comprehension with Multigenre Text Sets*. New York: Scholastic.

Nores, M., C. R. Belfield, W. S. Barnett, and L. J. Schweinhart. 2005. "Updating the Economic Impacts of the High/Scope Perry Preschool Program." *Educational Evaluation and Policy Analysis* 27(3): 245–261.

Nussbaum, A. D., and C. S. Dweck. 2008. "Defensiveness vs. Remediation: Self-Theories and Modes of Self-Esteem Maintenance." *Personality and Social Psychology Bulletin* 34: 599–612.

Nystrand, M. 2006. "Research on the Role of Classroom Discourse as it Affects Reading Comprehension." *Research in the Teaching of English* 40(4): 393–412.

Nystrand, M., with A. Gamoran, R. Kachur, and C. Prendergast. 1997. *Opening Dialogue: Understanding the Dynamics of Language and Learning in the English Classroom*. New York: Teachers College.

Oliner, S. P., and P. M. Oliner. 1988. *The Altruistic Personality: Rescuers of Jews in Nazi Europe*. New York: The Free Press.

Olson, R. L. 2003. "Strange Things You Likely Didn't Know." http://www.robinsweb.com/humor/strange_things.html.

Osborne, J., and C. Chin. 2010. "The Role of Discourse in Learning Science." In *Educational Dialogues: Understanding and Promoting Productive Interaction*, eds. K. Littleton and C. Howe. New York: Routledge.

Perner, J., U. Frith, A. M. Leslie, and S. R. Leekam. 1989. "Exploration of the Autistic Child's Theory of Mind: Knowledge, Belief, and Communication." *Child Development* 60(3): 689.

Perry, B. D. 2010. *Born for Love: Why Empathy is Essential—and Endangered.* New York: HarperCollins.

Peskin, J., and J. W. Astington. 2004. "The Effects of Adding Metacognitive Language to Story Texts." *Cognitive Development* 19(2): 253.

Peterson, C., N. Park, and M. E. P. Seligman. 2005. "Orientations to Happiness and Life Satisfaction: The Full Life Versus the Empty Life." *Journal of Happiness Studies* 6: 25–41.

Peterson, C. C., and M. Siegal. 2000. "Insights into Theory of Mind from Deafness and Autism." *Mind and Language* 15(1): 123.

Phillips, W. S., S. Baron-Cohen, and M. Rutter. 1998. "Can Children with Autism Understand Intentions?" *British Journal of Developmental Psychology* 16: 337–348.

Piaget, J. 1932. *The Moral Judgement of the Child.* London: Routledge.

Pierro, A., L. Mannetti, E. De Grada, S. Livi, and A. W. Kruglanski. 2003. "Autocracy Bias in Informal Groups Under Need for Closure." *Personality and Social Psychology Bulletin* 29: 405–417.

Plaks, J. E., C. S. Dweck, S. J. Stroessner, and J. W. Sherman. 2001. "Person Theories and Attention Allocation: Preferences for Stereotypic Versus Counterstereotypic Information." *Journal of Personality and Social Psychology* 80(6): 876–893.

Ray, K. W., with L. Cleaveland. 2004. *About the Authors: Writing Workshop with Our Youngest Writers.* Portsmouth, NH: Heinemann.

Reilly, M. A. 2008. "Finding the Right Words: Art Conversations and Poetry." *Language Arts* 86(2): 99–107

Rex, L. A., and M. C. Nelson. 2004. "How Teachers' Professional Identities Position High-Stakes Test Preparation in Their Classrooms." *Teachers College Record* 106(6): 1288–1331.

Ryan, R. M., and E. L. Deci. 2006. "Self-Regulation and the Problem of Human Autonomy: Does Psychology Need Choice, Self-Determination, and Will?" *Journal of Personality* 74(6): 1557–1586.

Saunders, W. M., and C. Goldenberg. 1999. "Effects of Instructional Conversations and Literature Logs on Limited- and Fluent-English-Proficient Students' Story Comprehension and Thematic Understanding." *Elementary School Journal* 99(4): 277–301.

Schultz, D., C. Izard, and B. Ackerman. 2000. "Children's Anger Attribution Bias: Relations to Family Environment and Social Adjustment." *Social Development* 9: 284–301.

Schwarz, B. B., N. Prusak, and R. Hershkowitz. 2010. "Argumentation and Mathematics." In *Educational Dialogues: Understanding and Promoting Productive Interaction*, eds. K. Littleton and C. Howe. New York: Routledge.

Schweinhart, L. J., J. Montie, Z. Xiang, W. S. Barnett, C. R. Belfield, and M. Nores. 2005. *Lifetime Effects: The High/Scope Perry Preschool Study Through Age 40.* Ypsilanti, MI: High/Scope.

Schweinhart, L. J., and C. R. Wallgren. 1993. "Effects of a Follow-Through Program on School Achievement." *Journal of Research in Childhood Education* 8(1): 43–56.

Schweinhart, L. J., and D. P. Weikart. 1998. "Why Curriculum Matters in Early Childhood Education." *Educational Leadership* 55(6): 57.

———. 1999. "The Advantages of High/Scope: Helping Children Lead Successful Lives." *Educational Leadership* 57(1): 76.

Seligman, M. E. P., and S. Nolen-Hoeksma. 1987. "Explanatory Style and Depression." In *Psychopathology: An Interactional Perspective*, eds. D. Magnusson and A. Ohman. Orlando, FL: Academic Press.

Shah, J. Y., A. W. Kruglanski, and E. P. Thompson. 1998. "Membership Has Its (Epistemic) Rewards: Need for Closure Effects on In-Group Bias." *Journal of Personality and Social Psychology* 75: 383–393.

Sharp, C. 2008. "Theory of Mind and Conduct Problems in Children: Deficits in Reading the 'Emotions of the Eyes.'" *Cognition and Emotion* 22(6): 1149–1158.

Sheeber, L. B., C. Johnston, M. Chen, C. Leve, H. Hops, and B. Davis. 2009. "Mothers' and Fathers' Attributions for Adolescent Behavior: An Examination in Families of Depressed, Subdiagnostic, and Nondepressed Youth." *Journal of Family Psychology* 23(6): 871-881. doi: 10.1037/a0016758.

Sheppard, L. A. 2002. "The Hazards of High-Stakes Testing." *Issues in Science and Technology* 19(2): 53.

Shih, M., and T. L. Pittinsky. 1999. "Stereotype Susceptibility: Identity Salience and Shifts in Quantitative Performance." *Psychological Science* 10(1): 80.

Smith, E. R., R. W. Tyler, and the Evaluation Staff. 1942. *Appraising and Recording Student Progress.* New York: Harper and Brothers.

Snyder, J., A. Cramer, J. Afrank, and G. R. Patterson. 2005. "The Contributions of Ineffective Discipline and Parental Hostile Attributions of Child Misbehavior to the Development of Conduct Problems at Home and School." *Developmental Psychology* 41: 30–41.

Sodian, B., Hulsken, C., and Thoermer, C. 2003. "The Self and Action in Theory of Mind Research." *Consciousness and Cognition* 12(4): 777.

Solomon, Y. 2008. *Mathematical Literacy: Developing Identities of Inclusion.* New York: Routledge.

Soorya, L. V., & D. Halpern. 2009. "Psychosocial Interventions for Motor Coordination, Executive Functions, and Socialization Deficits in ADHD and ASD." *Primary Psychiatry* 16(1): 48–54.

Soter, A. O., I. A. Wilkinson, P. K. Murphy, L. Rudge, K. Reninger, and M. Edwards. 2008. "What the Discourse Tells Us: Talk and Indicators of High-Level Comprehension." *International Journal of Educational Research* 47(6): 372–391.

Steele, C. M., and J. Aronson. 1995. "Stereotype Threat and the Intellectual Test Performance of African-Americans." *Journal of Personality and Social Psychology* 69(5): 797–811.

Steig, W. 1982. *Doctor De Soto.* New York: Farrar, Straus and Giroux.

Stojanovich, L., and D. Marisavljevich. 2008. "Stress as a Trigger of Autoimmune Disease." *Autoimmunity Reviews* 7(3): 209–213.

TeacherVision. n.d. "Character Traits." http://www.teachervision.fen.com/writing/resource/2669.html.

Thirty Schools Tell Their Story: Each School Writes of Its Participation in the Eight-Year Study. 1942. New York: Harper and Brothers.

Thorkildsen, T. A. 2000. "The Way Tests Teach: Children's Theories of How Much Testing Is Fair in School." In *Education, Culture, and Values, Vol. III: Classroom Issues: Practice, Pedagogy, and Curriculum,* eds. M. Leicester, C. Modgil and S. Modgil, 61–79. London: Falmer.

Topping, K. J., and S. Trickey. 2007a. "Collaborative Philosophical Inquiry for Schoolchildren: Cognitive Gains at 2-Year Follow-Up." *British Journal of Educational Psychology* 77(4): 787–796.

———. 2007b. "Collaborative Philosophical Enquiry for School Children: Cognitive Effects at 10–12 Years." *British Journal of Educational Psychology* 77(2): 271–288. doi: 10.1348/000709906x05328.

Tovani, C. 2000. *I Read It, but I Don't Get It: Comprehension Strategies for Adolescent Readers.* Portland, ME: Stenhouse.

Trickey, S., and K. J. Topping. 2004. "'Philosophy for Children': A Systematic Review." *Research Papers in Education* 19(3): 365–380.

————. 2006. "Collaborative Philosophical Enquiry for School Children." *School Psychology International* 27(5): 599–614. doi: 10.1177/0143034306073417.

Troyer, L., and R. Youngreen. 2009. "Conflict and Creativity in Groups." *Journal of Social Issues* 65(2): 409–427.

Turner, R. H., and L. Killian. 1957. *Collective Behaviour*. Englewood Cliffs, NJ: Prentice Hall.

van den Branden, K. 2000. "Does Negotiation of Meaning Promote Reading Comprehension? A Study of Multilingual Primary School Classes." *Reading Research Quarterly* 35: 426–443.

Volet, S., M. Vauras, and P. Salonen. 2009. "Self- and Social Regulation in Learning Contexts: An Integrative Perspective." *Educational Psychologist* 44(4): 215–226.

Vygotsky, L. S. 1978. *Mind in Society: The Development of Higher Psychological Processes.* Cambridge, MA: Harvard University Press.

Watson, A. C., C. L. Nixon, A. Wilson, and L. Capage. 1999. "Social Interaction Skills and Theory of Mind in Young Children." *Developmental Psychology* 35: 386–391.

Week, The. 2010. Einstein quotation. September 24.

Wegerif, R. 2007. *Dialogic Education and Technology: Expanding the Space of Learning.* New York: Springer.

Wentzel, K. R. 1994. "Relations of Social Goal Pursuit to Social Acceptance, Classroom Behavior, and Perceived Social Support." *Journal of Educational Psychology* 86: 173–182.

————. 1997. "Student Motivation in Middle School: The Role of Perceived Pedagogical Caring." *Journal of Educational Psychology* 89: 411–419.

White House. 2011. "Education: Guiding Principles." The White House. http://www.whitehouse.gov/issues/education.

Wilkes, S. 1994. *One Day We Had to Run: Refugee Children Tell Their Stories in Words and Paintings.* Minneapolis: Lerner.

Williams, R. G., and M. Williams. 2005. *Brothers in Hope: The Story of the Lost Boys of Sudan.* New York: Lee and Low.

Woolley, A. W., C. F. Chabris, A. Pentland, N. Hashmi, and T. W. Malone. 2010. "Evidence for a Collective Intelligence Factor in the Performance of Human Groups." *Science* 330(6004): 686–688. doi: 10.1126/science.1193147.

Yackel, E., P. Cobb, and T. Wood. 1991. "Small-Group Interactions as a Source of Learning Opportunities in Second-Grade Mathematics." *Journal for Research in Mathematics Education* 22(5): 390–408.

Yanoff, E. 2007. "Inquiry and Ideological Becoming in First Grade Literature Discussions." PhD diss., University at Albany-SUNY.

Index